"Everyday life is filled with situations that require the art of persuasion. From negotiating a raise to selling a product. From winning a political debate to getting your kids to do their homework. In every situation, you can choose how to approach the other person and what language to use. Lee Carter gives you a road map to making choices that will help you get what you want. Through real-world examples and extensive research, she has created simple tools that you can put to use to win hearts and minds.

"Effective communication starts with the ability to empathize deeply with your audience. In *Persuasion*, Lee explains what empathy is, why it matters, and how to use it to craft persuasive messages. Filled with examples and case studies, this book takes complex concepts and makes them easy to understand, and readily applicable to everyday life."

—Michael Maslansky, CEO, maslansky + partners,
and author of *Language of Trust*

"I can't think of a time when understanding the art and science of persuasion was more important than right now. This book is academic in its comprehensive approach. It's practical in how the reader can and should benefit from every lesson. It's so loaded with essential insight that I put my highlighter down after the first chapter—there was yellow on every page. As an occasional competitor, I shouldn't admit this, but the 'Persuasion Plan Workbook' is so essential to effective communication that I plan to steal it and use it for my clients immediately."

—Dr. Frank I. Luntz, author of *Words That Work*

"As this engaging book makes clear, what we have in common is often much more powerful than the differences that divide us. Building empathy and trust, rather than trying to be 'right,' offers a path toward positive change—on an individual level and for our culture at large."

—Scott Barry Kaufman, PhD, host of *The Psychology Podcast*
and author of *Transcend*

"Don't let the title fool you—this book is as much about listening as it is talking. Lee Carter explains how if you want someone to listen to you, you have to start by listening to them. If you want to know how to shift someone's mind-set, this practical book will help you see that the key ingredient is actually empathy."

—J. Stuart Ablon, PhD, associate professor at Harvard Medical School and author of *Changeable*

"As Lee Carter rightly points out, nobody today can afford to be a persuasion amateur. The very connections that sustain us and the aspirations that elevate us are at stake. Fortunately, she has created this smart playbook for a more effective, and far more human, approach to communication."

—Matthew DiGirolamo, chief communications officer, L'Oréal USA

"In the world of politics, Lee sees the entire playing field. This book will teach you to tell your story for maximum impact."

—Mitchell M. Roschelle, partner at PricewaterhouseCoopers

"In this compelling book, Lee gives us a road map for how to climb out of the empathy chasm. For people who long to find the place of commonality where meaningful change can happen, this is the book."

—Sharon Callahan, CEO, TBWA\Worldhealth

"In *Persuasion*, Lee Carter puts a science behind the art of persuasion. She gives clear instruction on how to effect change through communication. Everyone from CEOs to schoolteachers, parents to pastors, will find this book deeply helpful. Many of the largest corporations in the world hire Lee Carter to help them communicate effectively. In *Persuasion*, she shares her best advice with us. If you want to communicate in a way that leads to change, read this book and apply it."

—J. Josh Smith, pastor of Prince Avenue Baptist Church and author of *Preaching for a Verdict*

PERSUASION

PERSUASION

Convincing Others When
Facts Don't Seem to Matter

LEE HARTLEY CARTER

A TarcherPerigee Book

tarcherperigee
an imprint of Penguin Random House LLC
Penguinrandomhouse.com

Most Tarcher/Penguin books are available at special quantity discounts for bulk purchase for
sales promotions, premiums, fund-raising, and educational needs. Special books or book excerpts also
can be created to fit specific needs. For details, write: SpecialMarkets@penguinrandomhouse.com.

Library of Congress Cataloging-in-Publication Data
Names: Carter, Lee Hartley, author.
Title: Persuasion: convincing others when facts no longer seem to matter /
Lee Hartley Carter.
Description: [New York, NY] : TarcherPerigee, [2019] | Includes
bibliographical references and index.
Identifiers: LCCN 2019010664| ISBN 9780143133476 (hardcover) |
ISBN 9780525505273 (ebook)
Subjects: LCSH: Persuasion (Psychology) | Public relations.
Classification: LCC BF637.P4 C38 2019 | DDC 153.8/52—dc23
LC record available at https://lccn.loc.gov/2019010664
p.   cm.

Printed in Canada
1 3 5 7 9 10 8 6 4 2

Book design by Laura K. Corless

To my family, without whom nothing is possible

And to D, forever thankful for 3A and 3B

CONTENTS

PART 5: OWNERSHIP

PERSUASION

INTRODUCTION

WHEN FACTS DON'T MATTER

Today, on the news and in social media, there is much bemoaning that "facts no longer matter." By that, people mean that in a world where we have "alternative truth" and "truthiness" and consistent falsehoods being disseminated, facts no longer have the power to change minds. But I have to let you in on an industry secret: they never did.

In 1972, *after* news of the Watergate break-in made headlines, Richard Nixon still won reelection by a landslide because the facts at the time were open to interpretation. Just three years later, researchers at Stanford did the first study proving that people cling to their irrational opinions, even in the face of irrefutable evidence that they are wrong.* The hundreds of studies that followed prove that people actually dig their heels in when presented with facts that contradict their beliefs. If you want to change minds, facts alone have never been enough.

---

* Lee Ross, Mark R. Lepper, and Michael Hubbard, "Perseverance in Self-Perception and Social Perception: Biased Attributional Processes in the Debriefing Paradigm," *Journal of Personality and Social Psychology* 32, no. 5 (December 1975): 880–92.

The reasons are rooted in behavioral science. At a biological level our brains aren't hardwired to look for facts. Instead we rapidly and automatically process opinions we agree with *as if* they are facts. In the study "That's My Truth: Evidence for Involuntary Opinion Confirmation,"[*] researchers Michael Gilead, Moran Sela, and Anat Maril showed not only that our opinions are change-resistant, but that we actually *involuntarily* reject facts that contradict our existing opinions.

To compound this, all humans suffer from confirmation bias. We search for information that confirms our opinions. And we cherry-pick the facts that support our point of view. Here is a cartoon that really gets to the heart of this.

Our desire to confirm our existing beliefs also leads us to minimize or ignore data that doesn't fit our preferred view of the world. We can quickly dismiss factual information that does not agree with our worldview by labeling the new facts as somehow erroneous or limited. Said another way (shamelessly stealing from a former colleague): when confronted with facts that don't fit inside our frame,

* Michael Gilead, Moran Sela, and Anat Maril, "That's My Truth: Evidence for Involuntary Opinion Confirmation," *Social Psychological and Personality Science* (April 2018): doi: 10.1177/1948550618762300.

we throw away the facts and keep the frame (which is easier and less ego-threatening than getting a new frame).

But people don't just reject evidence that challenges their beliefs, they go even further. Studies of the often-quoted backfire effect demonstrate that when people reject evidence they don't like, their support for their original position gets stronger. In "Why Facts Don't Change Our Minds,"* Elizabeth Kolbert writes that scientists have deduced that the vaunted human capacity for reason may have more to do with winning arguments than with thinking straight: "Providing people with accurate information doesn't seem to help; they simply discount it."

Reading all this might make you feel hopeless. Don't be. All this tells us is that facts alone won't set us free. They won't tell our story. And they won't change hearts and minds. Decision-making is rarely a rational process. If you want to truly connect with others and shift their thinking, their behavior, their buying habits, or their voting practices, you must engage in a process that goes far beyond hitting them with statistics or study results.

This book is about persuading people to change their minds. It's not about appealing to your base or preaching to your choir. It's about engaging with someone who doesn't yet know you, agree with you, or sometimes even like you. It's about the very difficult challenge of overcoming your audience's human instinct to stick to their existing position. It is about giving people a reason to listen and then providing them with the right information in the right way so they can alter their existing point of view.

---

* Elizabeth Kolbert, "Why Facts Don't Change Our Minds," *The New Yorker*, February 27, 2017; https://www.newyorker.com/magazine/2017/02/27/why-facts-dont-change -our-minds.

All success, in life and in business, is based on the skill of persuasion. Put simply, you can have the best product, the best plan, the best policy, but if you're not telling your story in a way that connects and resonates with your audience, none of that matters. You will not persuade people to choose your company or follow your lead.

My question to you—and often to my clients—is, Which is more important: having a good story to tell, or telling your story well? Most people will immediately say that having a good story to tell is much more important. They will say that what matters is being a good company, having a good product, doing a good job. I agree that those things are important. But are they enough? Does the best product always win in the marketplace? Does the best strategy always work in practice? How you tell your story is just as important as having that good story to tell. My job and the job of my firm is to ensure that companies, issues, and people who have an important point to get across are able to tell their story in the best way possible. That is what persuasion is all about.

On election night 2016 I wasn't home like millions of Americans, glued to the TV, waiting to see if their strongest hopes or deepest fears would transpire. Instead I was in full hair and makeup, sitting in front of the cameras at Fox News. Because even though all of the network's polls suggested that Hillary Clinton would be our first female president, the anchors and viewers wanted to know if there was a chance that what *my* eighteen months of research had been predicting would be correct: that Trump would take the White House.

Regardless of how that statement makes you feel, regardless of whether you wanted me to be right or whether *I* wanted me to be right, the fact is that I was. And I was the outlier.

How was I able to see it coming when women across the nation were wearing suffragette white to their polling stations and Stephen Colbert had shirtless dancers lined up? Because I knew, based on my years of experience in the field of persuasive language, that Donald J. Trump had done exactly what it takes to get what he wanted—and Secretary Clinton had not. Post-election studies have confirmed it. He won, not because of low voter turnout among Democrats but because one in four white male Democrats who voted for Barack Obama switched parties. He won because he had mastered persuasion.

Leading up to the election, MSNBC, CNN, and Fox aired my firm's research on virtually every major speech, debate, and advertisement throughout the election process. What became clear was that Trump was penetrating because he viscerally understood the art of persuasion.

It's important to acknowledge that looking back at the 2016 race is emotional. No matter what side of the aisle you sit on, you will find it hard to look objectively at what happened in the election and why. And for all the reasons I have just outlined, it is hard for anyone who didn't support Trump to accept any data that argues he did things well.

There is also nothing more frustrating than watching from the sidelines as someone you support fails to effectively make their case for something you believe in—whether it's a candidate who loses, a local initiative that fails, or a piece of legislation you wish had more support. Have you ever closed the paper or turned off the news, full of frustration, and said, "It's so simple! Why can't they sell [universal health care/climate reform/immigration reform/bike lanes] better?!"

It's equally important to point out that when I talk about what worked for Donald Trump, I focus on the way he told his story to the public. In my mind, his tweets and demonstrated untruths were never the key to his success. And my approach to persuasion is based on telling the best version of your actual story—based on real facts and accurate information.

But if we take the emotion out of it and examine it like social and language scientists, then I ask you to think about what made the Trump candidacy successful. Trump was able to engage millions of voters because he understood what a significant portion of the public wanted to hear. He knew how his target voters felt. He knew what mattered to them. And he found the most effective way to appeal to them: he built a simple, clear master narrative that his audience could remember and repeat. It was supported by three narrative pillars, policies we could all remember and repeat. Love him or hate him, you knew exactly what his campaign stood for.

For the last twenty-five years, maslansky + partners has been at the forefront of studying how the words, messages, and stories that brands choose determine their place in the market. Because there is nothing more frustrating than seeing a group of brilliant people who have devoted years to creating something to help their consumers be unable to persuade anyone to try whatever it is. Frequently they struggle because they have been relying on facts alone to tell their story, or they hope that simply having made the best product will be enough.

It isn't.

So my job is to recognize, decode, and create impactful language for companies from Visa to PepsiCo, from ExxonMobil to Starbucks, to ensure their success. My firm's work has won numerous awards, but even more important to me, we have been able to help some of the world's best companies communicate on some of their most important challenges. And while the facts don't matter on their own, I am proud to help clients find the right way to present, frame, prioritize, and communicate them so that they can achieve their goals. And at the end of the day, that's what persuasion is all about—it's having the tools you need to be heard.

Long before I was president of a communications company I was fascinated by language. I remember realizing in high school that there really are no true synonyms. I used to torture my family and guests at our dinner table by asking them what the difference was between a geek, a nerd, a dweeb, and a loser. It was clear to me that while those words might be used interchangeably, each individual word actually describes a distinct cluster of traits and draws some pretty different images to our mind's eye.

It was this ability to parse the distinctions we make automatically that helped our firm to brand VIA, Starbucks' instant coffee. When VIA was getting ready to be launched, it wasn't catching on as the company had hoped. Management came to our firm to find out why. From their perspective, they were offering their customers even greater access and ease. But when we looked at the product from the consumer's perspective, it turned out the words *instant coffee* conjured exactly what people spend money at Starbucks to get *away* from. So we rebranded it as "VIA ready brew: Starbucks in an instant." After we changed up the words, consumers were no longer picturing the instant coffee of their childhoods; instead they were picturing getting their Starbucks coffee quickly and easily. This is now hailed as one of the most successful launches in consumer-packaged goods and is taught as part of a case study at Harvard Business School.

Mastering the skill of persuasion is vital for everyone. While I assume you are reading this book because you want to persuade consumers of your products, or your colleagues or your boss, you have other roles and identities outside of the office where these skills equally come into play. Think about a political issue that is important to you, or attempting a home renovation with a partner, or getting a kid to do anything they don't want to do, and tell me that persuasion stops when you leave work. When you think about it, you will realize that you persuade every day—probably multiple times a day.

For that reason, I will be including examples from the corporate world, the political world, and even my personal world. Because whether you're trying to shift responsibilities in your household, get a project off the ground at work, get your kids to take greater initiative in their academics, or get your mother-in-law to back off on your life choices, the bedrock of all of it is persuasion.

Whatever particular story you are preparing to tell, I will break down for you the nine essential steps you must take to get what you want, with a workbook in the final section so that you can build your own Persuasion Plan right in these pages.

We begin in part one with ourselves, our proposal, our goal, making sure we are audacious in our thinking but relatably vulnerable in our self-assessment. These two qualities are the foundation of persuasion.

Then in part two, you will learn that in order to form a successful connection with your audience, you can't know them superficially as a group or category—for example, women under fifty, millennials, the town's school board. You need to spend time doing a deep, honest evaluation of those you're *really* talking to as human beings—their hopes, dreams, and fears—and then find an empathic connection with them.

Not so long ago it used to be that the role of marketers, communicators, and politicians was to fall in love with their target audience. We would spend time learning about our customers. What they did when they woke up. What kind of coffee they drank (or didn't drink). Through market research, we knew everything about them, and we loved everything we discovered. Fast-forward to today. We know more about our customers than we ever have before, and we love them less. In fact, if you are honest with yourself—do you even *like* them?

It seems like the more data we have, the less intimate we've become. As someone who mines and analyzes this data, I can say it's a huge problem. Frequently we give our clients information about their potential clients' preferences but hit a wall because we find we can't make them *care*. Persuading someone to give you what you want starts with intimately knowing that person and *caring* about who they are and what they need.

It doesn't stop with marketing. Think about the people with whom you disagree. Do you try to understand them first, or do you try to change them?

We are in an empathy crisis. Whether you are trying to persuade someone to switch detergents or political parties, it is vital to empathize with your audience, to share and understand their feelings. Instead, today we traffic in disgust. Nowhere is this more visible than in politics. The rhetoric of both parties is one of judgment, and then social media fans the flames.

Culturally, we're able to self-identify more than we ever have before. It used to be that if you wanted to watch the news, there were three networks and they pretty much told the same story. In the last twenty years, since the rise of CNN, that has changed. You can choose the news you want to watch that's tailored to you. But if I'm a conservative and I'm watching only Fox News, I'm just getting fed what I want to hear. Personally, as someone with a conservative background,

I watch liberal networks and read newspapers with opposing perspectives because I want to learn how people with other viewpoints are thinking, but that's not what most people do. If you're politically minded, chances are the only political conversations you're having are with people who agree with you. On Facebook, you hear only from people who are like you. On Twitter, you follow the people you want to hear from. Even in the real world we are able to tailor our neighborhood and schools to stay in our bubbles.

But if we talk only to people who are just like us, then we think that everyone agrees with us. Despite social media, which should give us the opportunity to connect with people all over the world, from a myriad of different backgrounds, studies show that over the last thirty years we have become *more* insular. There are studies that say that parents of both parties would be more upset if their children married someone of a different political affiliation than somebody of a different race or religion. While I think it's great that people don't care as much about marriage across race or religion anymore— seriously? For all the conversations saying we're open-minded, we're really only open-minded to those who agree with us.

So we will be slowing down in chapter 3 to learn what I have termed *active empathy*, a new approach to empathy that builds on the social science, neuroscience, and biology research to help you put empathy into practice to keep hearts and ears open.

This is critical because people often confuse persuasion and manipulation. I get it. Both are trying to have an impact on and modify the behavior of another human being. But manipulation is nefarious. Persuasion is not. Manipulation is fleeting. You can get someone to buy a bad product—once. Persuasion is about a long-term relationship based in integrity and rooted in empathy. The notion starts with, How do I get what I want? But in order to be effective it has to become, How I can deliver what they *need*? Persuasive dialogue begins with *them*, your audience. We all know the feeling of someone talking *at* us instead of *to* us: an ad telling you that your favorite product now comes with something you never wanted, sitting through a presentation at your child's school where you feel like not one of your questions is getting addressed, or going on a date where you aren't asked anything about yourself. On the flip side, think of those moments when you really connected with a brand, a presentation, a date; my guess is that the resonance happened because whoever was making you an offer made *you* feel understood.

In parts three and four I'll break down the nitty-gritty components of language strategy—authenticity, master narrative, proof points, visual language, and storytelling—so that you can build your own strategy and use it with confidence.

Then in part five I'll arm you with the skills you need to go the distance, in order to truly own your message and embody it, through any storm you encounter.

⸻

In the age when a voice of authority ruled, be it from the nightly news or from a consumer agency seal of approval, communication could be academic and still be effective. You could put out an ad and people bought into the promise. But now, when all opinions are crowd-sourced and an alternative narrative is available to anyone with a browser, you have to engage the emotional side of persuasion to reach your audience.

The era of subtlety is over.

Before, communication supported the brand; now communication *is* the brand. Before, the candidate sold a story; now the story sells the candidate. Before, your résumé positioned you; now your position upstages your résumé. These rules will define not only the next few decades in politics but which companies will survive and thrive. It's also going to impact our personal lives and dictate if we continue down our path of tribalism—congregating only with folks we agree with—or if we are able to come together as one and learn from one another.

Once you have mastered the simple steps of my persuasion process, you will be on your way to being able to persuade anyone of anything: to sign off on your budget, agree to your hire, buy your product, call you back—or even vote you president.

PART 1

YOU

1

LOOK BOLDLY BEYOND YOUR LIMITS

Vision without action is merely a dream. Action without vision just passes the time. Vision with action can change the world.

–JOEL BARKER

This is a book about effective communication. Yes, I am going to teach you how to get your ideas across so they become powerful realities, but before we get there, we want to make sure that the ideas you're trying to get across are the right ones. The best ones. The biggest ones.

In order to persuade, you first need to know exactly what you want to achieve. What you *really* want to achieve, not what you've been led to believe is practical or readily attainable. Not what others want for you. But your vision for yourself or your company or the organization you volunteer for on the issues that matter most.

When I sit down with a client to kick off any project, one of the first things I ask is "What are you hoping to accomplish?" Frequently, people will give us general goals, much as they would in a business plan. I like to get specific. I want to know *exactly* what success looks like to them. Because often we know in global terms what we need to accomplish, but for persuasion, it's just simply not enough to say, "I want to be more popular." With whom? "We want greater market share." In which market, with which product? "I want a promotion." To what position, making how much more? "We want more people to prevent climate change." Doing what? By when? Accomplishing persuasion relies on specificity. I want all the details. I like to be able to picture *exactly* what success looks like.

In our social media world, popularity or notoriety is readily available—but what if it's with a consumer base that doesn't actually need or can't afford your product? You could attain market share with a product that isn't cost-effective for you to manufacture. And how many people these days are given promotions with new titles that don't come with salary increases? These are just a few examples, but I want you to understand right away why this step of getting clear about your goals—going beyond being "liked"—is so vital.

SPECIFICITY

First, know that being able to answer these questions takes time. This isn't something we ever solve for a client in a single session. It takes thought. It takes reflection. It takes getting specific. Because if you can't be specific, you're likely not going to know what you need to do, your team won't know where you're going, and you won't know success when you see it. Without specifics, you are likely to fail.

When I was just out of college, my friend Glenn and I were having drinks and he asked me what my dream for the future was. I gave some sort of half answer: "Well, you know, to have a job I like. A husband I love. Hopefully a family." He looked at me with a cocked eyebrow and took another gulp of his drink. Then he said to me, "Lee, that's not a dream. A dream is specific. A dream is visual.

When I say, 'What's your dream?' I want you to be able to paint a picture of exactly what it is that you want." I sighed, looked down at my drink, and thought, *Man, that is scary. What if I'm specific and then I don't pull it off? What if I say this out loud and sound like an idiot?* I rolled my eyes and tried to change the subject.

Glenn put down his drink and looked me square in the eye and said, "Let me tell you about my dream. Fifteen years from now I will be on a boat fishing with my friends, pulling up to my dock, listening to Bob Seger. The wind will be in my hair. I will have caught three big fish. And my wife and daughter will be standing on the dock waiting for me. It will be an epic Saturday. And I will know, just know, that I made it." He said this with full confidence and no sense of irony. Guess who now has a boat he pulls up to the slip while listening to Bob Seger's "Hollywood Nights"? Glenn does.

I have thought of that evening so many times over the years. Eventually, using the process I'm about to outline for you, I have set and attained big goals for my career. Yet I have often been scared to do the same for my personal life. On a recent weekend away, I learned that many of my friends had the reverse problem. But whatever the case, whether it's your personal life or your professional life, setting those goals is the first step in getting what you want.

BEYOND POPULARITY

We were recently working with a top pharmaceutical company. It may not come as a surprise to you that since the last election cycle, pharmaceutical companies have been suffering from a reputation crisis around the pricing of their medications. And while there were good underlying reasons for the cost increases, a few bad actors in the industry had made pharma the poster child for excess (thanks,

Martin Shkreli). When we ran focus groups, people told us that they viewed *all* pharma companies as "greedy, charging way too much for drugs that cost them pennies to manufacture and profiting off others' misfortune." And my clients—many of whom had decided to work in the industry because they believed that they could make a big difference by finding cures and developing life-improving drugs— were shocked at what they heard. They really thought that they were the good guys—on the front lines of trying to cure diseases and save lives—while those other companies were the bad guys. All they needed to do was to show the difference.

But if they really wanted to rebuild a positive relationship with the consumer, the solution wasn't just to point out who was good and who was bad. We had to find a way to tell the company's story of innovation and cures that could help consumers see what the company already knew internally. To succeed, the corporate management couldn't just say, "We want to be viewed better." They needed to know *exactly* what they wanted to be viewed *as*—what their image should be. So we worked with them to try to understand what would actually move the needle. To do that, we needed to get at the question behind the question. Why do Americans mistrust pharmaceutical companies so much? After we did our research, it turned out the answer was surprisingly simple. People have no idea what pharmaceutical companies really do. They just thought they did.

Our data showed that consumers think pharma manufactures pills and sells them at huge markups. Consumers don't take into account clinical trials or research. They don't count the scientists involved. They don't consider any of the things that drive up the cost of drugs. Because in our culture, others get credit for all of pharma's research and development: charities and academic institutions have become the face of striving for cures. What is the first thing you do when one of your loved ones gets cancer or any other disease? It's likely this: Go to a fundraiser. Walk, run, or cycle for a cure. Donate to the charity. The last think you think is *I better send a letter to the CEOs of Pfizer, Merck, and Novartis to see what drugs they have in the pipeline.* Therein lay the problem.

To turn things around, we needed to persuade the influential consumers that pharmaceutical companies are more than pill manufacturers. That they are looking for cures each and every day—for the most serious medical conditions as well as for common ailments.

So it wasn't about being liked. Liked would have taken us on an unproductive tangent. It was about persuading consumers of pharma's intention to *help* them. That was a case that could be made with the tools I'm going to provide you with in parts three and four. Launching a campaign emphasizing their research and development increased their sales, improved their share price, and raised the money to develop the next medication to help people, which as far as pharma was concerned was what it was all about.

THINKING BEYOND THE OPTIONS IN FRONT OF YOU

As a child, I always played business. While other girls turned a blanket over a table into a house, I turned it into an ice cream shop or a post office or a bank. It didn't matter what the business was; what I enjoyed was providing an imaginary service and taking play money from my friends and putting it in my Fisher-Price cash register.

But in 2005 I was approaching thirty and wasn't happy in my job in the insurance industry. Nothing about where I was living or what I was doing felt like the right fit for me personally, even though everyone around me was telling me I had already broken the mold. I was the first woman in my family to choose to go to college and focus on building a career.

But my life was the result of exactly the kind of vague dreaming my friend had warned me about. I had wanted a career. I had one—in an industry I wasn't passionate about. I had wanted independence. I think I actually meant financial independence, but because I hadn't been specific, I was also living alone.

Because I had never taken the time to get clear about envisioning a life that incorporated everything I wanted—work that set me on fire, a relationship that would support my ambitions, a way to include motherhood that allowed for me to continue working—I was actually exactly what I had been afraid of becoming all those years ago when I applied to college: unfulfilled.

I knew I wanted more. But the answer wasn't right in front of me. It wasn't an option being presented to me by my then circumstances. It wasn't about being promoted or jumping to another insurance company, or getting more successful right where I was, doing what I'd been doing.

The change was going to take vision. It was going to take getting out of my comfort zone and imagining something for myself that wasn't obvious.

So I sat down and asked myself, *What do I love? What do I want more of in my life? What am I passionate about?*

These are also a questions I frequently ask clients. Because what you love is what you should be doing more of. This seems obvious, but it's also true in business. Think about companies with multiple divisions and revenue streams. At the end of 2018, Citigroup sold off its mortgage division to Cenlar because it realized that its focus on diversification, so popular in the nineties and aughts, had actually led to a dilution of its core focus and a decrease in profits. They looked at what they did best—commercial banking—and decided to embrace that and try to own more of that space.

If you want something because it genuinely excites you, you are going to be that much more persuasive because you are going to make a strong and passionate case for it. This is as true when you are trying to convince your community board to start a planting project as it is when my clients are bringing a new consumer product to market. Excitement—love—is contagious.

My answers were:

1. I love words and language.
2. I love politics.
3. I want to help people across clashing groups become more understanding of one another.

This was in 2005, right after George W. Bush was elected for the second time, and as close as we had all felt after 9/11, we were once again a country divided. As someone who split time between rural New Jersey and New York City, I felt very much at the center of that divide. The city had one set of politics, but my family and friends in the suburbs had another. I was moving between two communities of people I loved and respected who couldn't find a way to listen to each other.

So, now I had my three guiding principles: language, politics, and empathy. But that didn't describe any profession that I knew of.

Then I thought back to Glenn's advice and decided I wouldn't do it my way again. I wouldn't retrofit my ambition to match something I already knew about, something "fine." I would stay committed to my specific vision: I wanted a new job that somehow involved language, politics, and collaborative communication, even though I had no idea what that was.

HOW VISION INFORMS ACTION

Once I was clear about my commitment, my vision dictated my choices. Since nothing fit the bill where I was, I knew I needed to start broadening my horizons. I signed myself up for courses, lectures, and networking events. I bought books. I reached out to friends across the country. At every juncture, when I hesitated about signing up for the next mixer or sending the next email, I simply asked myself, *Is this action potentially moving me closer to my vision?* If my answer was yes, I pressed Send.

A few months later I found myself signing up for a conference in Charleston, South Carolina. It was called Renaissance Weekend and brought together the greatest minds in business, politics, and the arts. Everyone who attended had to speak and participate. Nobel laureates. Pulitzer Prize winners. Oscar-winning screenwriters. Congresspeople. A Supreme Court justice. I was in so far over my head. What did Lee Carter from small-town New Jersey have in common with an astronaut? What could I possibly add to a conversation with a former president? My insecurity started to get the best of me—until I heard one man speak. His name was Frank Luntz, and as he talked about the importance of language, messaging, and story in the 2004 election, I was mesmerized. He was one of the founding partners of maslansky + partners, and I knew—I just *knew*—I had found my next career.

But I had no experience in the field. I had the wrong degree. And I lived in New York City, not in Washington, D.C.

In the next chapter I'll share how I persuaded them to even interview me. But the point here is that without my specific vision, I wouldn't have even taken the steps that led me to that conference, and I wouldn't have recognized the opportunity when it arrived.

What would have happened if I didn't think beyond the scope of the options right in front of me? I would be sitting somewhere in an office park collecting a paycheck, doing something I hated, as so many people do. I would never have followed then senator Barack Obama through Iowa and New Hampshire. I would never have followed President Trump's rise from the escalator to the White House. And I would never have found myself on air, sitting next to one of my work idols, Maria Bartiromo, every week.

THE THREE BENEFITS OF VISION

In 2007, we had a client who wanted us to help him find the language of giving. When I asked him what his goal was, he said simply, "To save the world." His incredible and selfless goal was to get everyone in the world to give to something. We were very moved by his intention and wanted to make sure that this vision was translated into something specific that could actually be acted upon and have impact. As it stood, the goal was too broad to motivate. Give what? To whom? Why? Persuasion isn't just about language and message; it is equally about strategy. He knew that when you try to persuade people to do too much, you will paralyze them or, worse still, be ignored entirely. He wanted our help—not just with language but with redefining his vision to become concrete. Here are the three benefits of being clear about your vision.

BENEFIT 1. FOCUS

A specific vision will help you prioritize. You have only so much mental energy or time in a day and only so many resources. If you aren't crystal clear about what you are trying to accomplish, you will waste time on activities that aren't moving you forward. You can ask yourself, *Is this choice moving me closer to my vision?* If it isn't, it might be counterproductive.

For example, if your vision is to turn the tide politically, are you making time to talk to voters, meet with potential candidates, and volunteer? If your vision is opening a restaurant, but you haven't blocked out any time to look at spaces, meet with investors, or study the dining habits in your desired neighborhood, your vision isn't going to become a reality. Once you let your vision dictate your focus, devoting time and energy becomes easier.

This is especially true for companies. Once I have created a Persuasion Plan for a client, we always have to make sure companies have allocated enough resources to follow through on the plan. It's pointless for a company to say, "We are committing to greater transparency in our loan process," if they haven't also put the legal team in place to draft the new documents and seen to the training necessary to educate their employees.

Let's get back to my client who wanted to save the world. Our client had a big vision, but we needed him to focus. We talked through what impact he could have on the three groups he could target to inspire philanthropy: the wealthiest of the wealthy, corporations, and individuals like you and me. After going through this sorting exercise, he realized that he could have the greatest impact on the future if he started engaging young people while they were deciding what they wanted to do for the rest of their lives. Ultimately, he focused on the data that said if you engage college students in acts of generosity early, they will end up being altruistically focused throughout their lives.

We have seen the results of his efforts—more young people today want to work at nongovernmental organizations (NGOs) than they do at investment banks. We have college campuses more engaged than ever with volunteerism and fundraising. All because our client was able to harness his energies to a big, bold—but focused—vision.

BENEFIT 2. GETTING OTHERS ON BOARD

The second benefit of having a specific vision is that it motivates other people to help make it happen. Good leaders do this all the time. But it's just as true at home as at work.

For example, maybe you have set a goal of more family time. If you say to your family, "I want more family meals," they may smile and nod, they may even agree with you, but you still haven't communicated a specific vision they can collaborate on making a reality.

Instead if you say, "Okay, guys, I just read that kids who eat dinner with their parents at least three nights a week do much better at school and are more successful in the long term. That's what we want for you. So, Sunday, Tuesday, and Thursday, everyone needs to be at this table by seven p.m." That is a specific goal they can work with you to achieve. If you can't get them on board, no matter how strong your vision is, it will not happen. Most goals, especially business goals, require collaboration to be successful.

Nowhere has this been more important than in my role as president of maslansky + partners. In the late aughts, we realized that in order to continue to grow, we needed to resolve a key strategic issue. Internally we had been going in circles: Were we a language firm, a messaging firm, or a research firm? As a result, our marketing suffered because we could never agree on which aspect of our services to promote. My partners and I knew we had the answers for many of the challenges our clients faced, but our team wasn't coming along for the ride. Our team wanted to keep doing our primary type of research and focus on the core set of challenges we had historically addressed. But the partners saw bigger opportunities. This conflict led to something of an identity crisis.

Then, at an executive business course, I was tasked with thinking about a business challenge I wanted to solve. I realized right away that we'd never created a vision that we had shared with our team of what *we* wanted the firm to be. We had lost time trying to figure out if we were option a, b, or c, but perhaps instead we were a fourth thing, a new thing, something no one had seen before, a new way of serving clients.

What if the answer was leaning *into* what made us hard to categorize? We decided to organize our business around what we were already doing best—language strategy. We looked at the evolution of brand strategy and saw that over the previous decades, it had moved from logos to color schemes to customer service to the "experience"— the smell of a hotel lobby, the greeter at the store entrance.

Our business had a similar opportunity. We started as a firm that did research on public affairs issues to help clients communicate more effectively. Then we worked to help companies find the right language for new products and brands. Clients had pushed us to go further. They asked us to help their senior management communicate strategy. They looked for us to explain complex policies to customers and employees. They challenged us to use a new way of speaking to influence the internal culture of different organizations. And we realized that in an era with decreased attention spans and increased message clutter, the language companies use has never been more important. Language shapes virtually every aspect of how customers, prospects, employees, investors, and other stakeholders experience a company. Words shape the employee experience and the customer experience. We recognized that in many cases there is no budget for language strategy, just as in the past there had been no budget for brand strategy. We envisioned a time when language strategy would become an essential part of every company's business strategy. And today that vision guides us and shapes our own strategy.

The next step was to be clear to our staff about what we wanted to be. We painted a picture and encouraged our team to get comfortable being uncomfortable while we came up with new ways of applying what we do to different challenges.

Our vision enabled us to be more confident about our value and more comfortable engaging with clients in new ways. And the company grew. None of this would have been possible without expanding our vision beyond the options right in front of us. And none of it would have happened if our team hadn't been following through. Because it is them—and not just the partners—who are driving this growth.

BENEFIT 3. MOTIVATION

From time to time we all face burnout, discouragement, and frustration. Your vision will give you at least five things that will keep you going when the latest prototype of your design doesn't work, or there's a strike in your supply chain, or you just run out of inspiration.

When I was first developing the persuasion process for this book, there were days I had a hard time formalizing what we do as a business as we had been doing it all on instinct. A few times I was tempted to throw in the towel. To persevere I had to come back to my vision, why I believed we needed to share the steps to persuasion.

I believe in a vision in which we all know these fundamental skills and apply them routinely in our lives and workplaces. In that vision:

1. We will have better, less cynical conversations.
2. We will be open to different viewpoints.

3. We will listen respectfully to one another.
4. We will strengthen empathy.
5. We will have meaningful and lasting relationships with our customers and other target audiences.

I've learned that fear limits you and your vision. It serves as blinders to what may be just a few steps down the road for you. The journey is valuable, but believing in your talents, your abilities, and your self-worth can empower you to walk down an even brighter path. Transforming fear into freedom—how great is that? —SOLEDAD O'BRIEN

WHAT GETS IN THE WAY?

The number one challenge I see when clients, or even friends, have a desire to promote their ideas or goals is not that they're overreaching in their ambition but that their ambition is too small to be inspiring. If they're not inspired, how can they hope to inspire others? You can stop yourself from getting what you want before you've even gotten started. In my experience, there are three main pitfalls that get in our way. Be sure to look out for these in your own thinking.

PITFALL 1. SELF-TALK

The people in their twenties whom I mentor consistently suffer from talking themselves out of something before they've even begun. They are afraid that they don't have the right degree or contacts. If they have started down one path, they will talk about how hard it is to change industries. When Michelle Obama was a guest on Oprah's podcast, she talked about how when she set out her goals as the daughter of a water plant employee on the South Side of Chicago, she didn't have the edge. She didn't have the contacts or the experience; no one in her family had attended Ivy League schools or law school. She went on to share the same advice that I do. Life will change only when you stop looking for pragmatic reasons as to why your goal is unattainable.

The other common error is looking to past experience to give you the odds on your future success. No one's ever asked you to dance, so no one ever will. You haven't gotten pregnant, so you won't. You haven't won the school lottery, so your ticket won't get pulled out of the bowl. This attitude is understandable, but life doesn't work like that. The dance partners and the eggs and the tickets don't talk to one another. You start with fresh odds every time.

Negative self-talk is tempting because it can feel self-protective— even comforting. We think if we hammer home to ourselves all the reasons our vision is ludicrous, it won't hurt so much when someone else hurts us. But you can't create a protective callus of negativity.

Instead, you'll only undermine yourself. If you want to get what you want, if you want to start persuading people to give you what you want, you have to stop this cycle.

PITFALL 2. DEFERRING TO CYNICS

We all have at least one naysayer in our lives. For our clients, it's often their lawyers. For many people, it's their parents or spouses. "How are you going to have time for that?" "Are you crazy? You've got a secure job now, why shake things up?" "We have the lion's share of the market—this isn't the time to innovate!"

We had a client who wanted to set a goal of making the company water neutral by the year 2020. This would be a huge goal for any manufacturer, but this was a beverage company; water was necessary to make the product. So one by one, people around the organization told this executive why it was impossible. They asked, "What will happen if we don't meet the goal?" "Will the stock price tank?" Lawyers were fearful of the promise. Manufacturing plants were sure it was impossible. Finance said it would be too expensive. Even the environmental groups said that maybe, just maybe, they should push out the timeline. Or make the goal smaller. But this leader went out there and made the promise anyway, saying, "If we don't set the goal, it's never going to happen. And if we miss it, at least we will be better than we are today, and we will all have learned from it."

PITFALL 3. LOOKING OUTSIDE YOURSELF

This is self-sabotage masking as due diligence. These are the people who will ask everyone for advice until they find the one person who tells them no. Then they will say, "See, this was a bad idea." Of course, if you look hard enough, you will always find reasons why you won't get what you want, why what you're doing is improbable— or impossible. Hardly anything great ever achieved seemed like a slam dunk at the outset. J. K. Rowling, Oprah, Barack Obama—these weren't people you could have looked at in their youth and thought, *Oh yeah, of course, it's so obvious they're going to change the world.* I'm sure that if they had had the inkling then, the calling, they could have just asked around until someone said, "You know, I would put away that ambition and just get a regular day job. Something with a steady paycheck."

When we are afraid, it's human nature to want to validate the reasons to avoid risk. But giving in to fear keeps us from our best, negativity keeps us from achieving, and finding stories that reinforce our fears can paralyze us.

I'm not suggesting that you avoid research or that you not learn from your failures. I'm just saying that you can't let failures or cautionary tales define you.

Despite the fact that the economy is booming, communications firms have struggled. I would talk to my colleagues in other companies about our firm's vision for growth and they would discourage me. They would tell me about budgets being slashed, about an industry undergoing tremendous change. So long as I listened, I in turn stayed stuck. I stayed small in my thinking and we didn't grow. But once I stopped listening to everyone else and we leaned into our vision of meeting a niche need, things took off.

COURAGE

It's going to take one thing to avoid falling into these traps: courage. It will take tremendous bravery not to listen to authority figures and naysayers. It will be tough going at times to silence that voice of doubt inside your head. It will be hard to look at failures and, instead of being defined by them, learn from them. But if you want to win, you will have to. Otherwise the vision you create will be watered down and uninspiring to the point that even you won't want to follow through.

When Blake Mycoskie founded TOMS, it was based on a largely untested idea: that a company could be viable by charging a premium for their product if each purchase did direct social good. Absolutely no one thought it was a good idea. Blake started with 250 pairs in stock and had to sell his previous business to finance production. Today the company is valued at over $600 million. By committing to an audacious vision—ending shoelessness and the accompanying diseases for children in developing nations—he made his dream a reality. You can do the same.

I have a friend who is a doctor but felt the urge to do something more to promote breast cancer prevention. She had no political experience and a full-time job she was not prepared to quit. But her passion around the issue was authentic, and that resonated with her local government. She had been thinking she would have to quit medicine to have an impact, but once she let that self-imposed limitation go, she was able to expand her vision. She's now running her township committee on public health policy and spent a week in D.C. meeting with congresspeople as the new health legislation is drafted.

Think about it for a second. What kind of people do you want to vote for? What products do you want to buy? What kind of people do you want to hire? What stocks do you want to invest in? That's right—the visionaries. The optimists. When I am testing candidates' messaging, it's always the big ones that resonate.

One thing I have learned is that whether it's personal or professional, when you think big, you get genuinely excited about what you're going after, and that authentic excitement is much easier to communicate. So what is it that you want?

Do you want a great partner?

Do you want a whole new career?

Do you want to run for local office?

Do you want people to care—I mean really care—about an issue that is near to your heart: climate change, equal pay, or keeping a new development from happening in your community?

Do you want to change the culture in your company?

Do you want to launch the next blockbuster medicine?

What is it that you want—*really*? Not what your girlfriends have told you is "realistic." Not what accounting has told you is "feasible." Not what HR has conditioned you to think is "reasonable." Not what regulatory says you "are allowed to say." Not what finance has told you is "within reach." As a culture, we have gotten really good at explaining why something *can't* happen, instead of explaining why it can. Great leaders don't do that. They think big; they dream big.

For you to do the same, the first step is carving out some time for yourself to daydream. To ask yourself, *What do I love? What drives me? What of that could I use to have an impact?* Take an inventory. When do you do your best thinking? At the gym? On a walk? While doing the dishes? Give yourself a break from your routine where your mind is cluttered with the next task you're trying not to forget. If your job is too consuming to make that space, you may need to get away— a hike alone on the weekend. Or even a trip. I find I do my best big thinking when I've gotten out of my routine or, even better, my comfort zone.

When you have gotten clear about what exactly it is you want, write it down. An auto company came to me recently because no one really knew what the company stood for anymore. They had no over-arching vision. So our team spoke with everyone who was instrumental in making their cars—the engineers, the designers—and wrote down what they valued about their work.

The theme that clearly emerged was mobility. They saw themselves as providing a service by getting people safely and efficiently though their lives. We were then able to expand their mission in two directions. Instead of a car company, they could be a mobility company, investing in aeronautics and mass transit solutions. For the community, it meant an investment in upward mobility—engineering scholarships and science initiatives. Once you write it down, mere inclinations become data points.

YOUR TURN FOR ACTION

What is your biggest, your best, your brashest, your boldest wish? Get out a piece of paper and a pen. Yes, this is an analogue exercise, but research has shown that for this kind of thinking, the physical act of writing activates the brain in a way that typing doesn't. Now write down: What is it I want?

1. **Take your time.** Your first answer will probably need amplification.

2. **Be specific.** Visualize it. Every detail.

3. **Don't be embarrassed.** As a child I thought it would be so cool to be Barbara Walters, but I spent twenty years saying I couldn't. It was only when I silenced that voice that I became a news correspondent.

4. **Be able to measure your success.**

   a. *If it's personal*: Know how you're going to measure success so you can know how far you need to go. For the mother who wanted more family dinners, is the goal seven nights a week? Two? What does success look like? When will you evaluate? Do you check in after six months? Does it carry over to other things? Is it really about being heard and respected? Then you have to go back to your visions. That can be circular.

   b. *If it's a product*: If you're the manager for an annuity or you're selling something you made on Etsy, what defines success? For some people, it's simply "I get it done and to market." For others, it's "Five people buy it." For some of our clients, it needs to be the number one bestselling product. For some, it's all of the above.

   c. *If it's a company:* The metric can be turning the company's reputation around, from least respected to most respected. Or if this is about changing something within company culture, there may be internal metrics. How many sick days are people taking? How much turnover is there? How are people rating their job satisfaction? Set goals and metrics by which you'll meet them.

5. **Write your own personal mission statement.** Now take a moment to pull it all together. Write it down. Refer to it often. This is going to be your north star as you weather the persuasion storm that will come.

2

GETTING REAL WITH YOURSELF

Everything I was told should be my greatest insecurities, my weaknesses, my biggest roadblocks—everything that I've been labeled: short, nerdy, skinny, weak, impulsive, ugly, tomboy, poor, rebel, loud, freak, crazy— turned out to be my greatest strengths. I didn't become successful in spite of them. I became successful because of them. —AJ MENDEZ

Have you ever walked away from a social setting thinking you couldn't stand to be part of the conversation for another minute because the person you were speaking to seemed fake? How many times have you rolled your eyes at an advertisement for a skin cream that promised to be the fountain of youth? Walked away from a job interview saying, "I just can't put my finger on it, but I don't trust that person"? Closed a brochure about a new financial product thinking that there is just no way that it can perform at that pace with no downside? We live in a society that strives for perfection but celebrates authenticity. And there's a problem with that. These two concepts are frequently at odds with each other. In this chapter, I'll be covering the fundamental principles of authenticity and showing how they apply to people, products, and politicians alike. And I'll explain how acknowledging vulnerability in marketing can sometimes be the savviest strategy.

You and the person you're trying to persuade live in the same reality. It's critical not to set the wrong expectations based on who you *think* your customer is looking for. If you come at them trying to convince them that you are something other than what they perceive you to be, you will come across as untrustworthy, and that is almost impossible to come back from. Nothing kills a brand's story faster than a contradiction.

But let's be clear: Persuasion isn't convincing someone that you are something that you're not. Persuasion is about finding an authentic story that will change beliefs or behaviors. So don't promise innovation if you're just meeting a need. Don't tell your date you love dogs if you really don't. Don't tell your boss you're ready for a managerial role if you're actually just getting up to speed. If there's a perception gap between how you see yourself and how the person you are trying to persuade sees you, you will have a problem.

But this also doesn't mean that authenticity can't be part of your advantage. For years Avis was the number two car rental company in the country behind Hertz. They couldn't advertise that they were the best or rated number one at anything. There was no breaking Hertz's supremacy, so finally Avis leaned into it. "Avis: We try harder." It was a sleek slogan that acknowledged their position and also told the customer that there was an upside to going with number two. It worked: the company became profitable for the first time in a decade.

Whether or not you personally responded to Trump's messaging as he campaigned for office, my research showed that to many voters he came across as authentic and unfiltered. He owned his lack of political experience without apologizing for it. His audience felt they could trust him because he would "tell it like it is." When I tested his speeches in parts of the country where the economy had never fully recovered from the crash, people didn't want to be told, "We have come so far, but there is a long way to go," because that did not reflect their experience. They didn't have jobs, so they didn't feel that they had come far and they certainly didn't want to be told that there was still "a long way" to go. They wanted solutions *now.* When he reflected their perspective back to them—that they wanted to go back to work, that they needed jobs in America, that the government *had* been letting them down by allowing jobs to be moved overseas, and that they deserved better—they felt validated.

Another way of thinking about authenticity is vulnerability. Dr. Brené Brown, a research professor who has spent the past two decades studying shame and vulnerability, defines vulnerability as "uncertainty, risk, and emotional exposure."

Now you may think, *Those qualities are the opposite of what I want to bring to persuasion. I want to be certain going in that I'm going to win, with low risk and low potential for emotional exposure.* But think about people who have persuaded you—to support them, vote for them, or buy their product. If there is a vulnerability there and they acknowledge it, it's so much more powerful than trying to pretend it doesn't exist. For all his boasting and bluster, Trump openly acknowledged his lack of political experience, but then reframed it as a plus to his supporters.

If someone is running for office without experience . . . he or she better acknowledge it. If someone is asking you to stop using an established brand and take a chance on a start-up, they better address that you are taking a risk with them. If a woman is lobbying your company to add paid paternity leave, she needs to say that she might not be the obvious spokesperson for this issue and then go on to explain why that's a strength. If a company has messed up, they better acknowledge they have if they want to earn back trust, which is exactly what this chapter is about—how to use your vulnerabilities to strengthen your argument, without spinning them into something that rings false to your audience.

AUTHENTICITY VERSUS THINKING BIG

One question I get all the time: Are authenticity and thinking big at odds with each other? Absolutely not. Barack Obama was only a one-term senator when he ran for president. He presented his relative newness to the partisan, lobby-beholden world of Washington as a strength and leaned into his recent work as a community organizer to position himself as someone who understood the American people "on the ground."

When I first learned a job that focuses on language, message, and persuasion even existed, it would have been so easy to let my limitations tell me that there was no way to persuade these people to interview me. Instead, I got scrappy. I emailed. I called. I mailed letters. I asked everyone I knew if they had a way for me to get in. Then one evening one of my closest friends ended up at a dinner with the co-founders of the firm; she told them that I was obsessed with what they did. They happened to be opening a New York office and—boom!—I had my interview.

But if I had gone in and said, "I'm a perfect writer, an established researcher, and the most trusted adviser to top-level executives you will ever meet," I would have been laughed out of the room.

Instead, I acknowledged, "I might not have the obvious experience, but I know people. In my years in the insurance industry I learned how to understand their worldview and communicate to it." I made sure to emphasize that I was a sociology major—that was one of my proof points, which we'll talk more about later. I wrapped up by telling the hiring team that my passion for understanding the way people interact and my obsession with language made me the right candidate for the job. My pitch was honest, it owned up to my short-comings, and yet it triumphantly positioned me.

VULNERABILITY IN CRISIS

Before the financial crisis of 2008, we had a client who was one of America's top national commercial banks—let's call them Bank Main Street. As part of our services, we performed a lot of market research, delving into the target consumers' spending and saving habits, asking questions like "What do you look for in a checking account?" and "What would incentivize you to sign up for a home equity line of credit?"

Then during the crisis, they bought one of the smaller banks that had made too many subprime loans and was in danger of going under. What transpired was that after the crisis, whenever we were having focus groups about personal finances in the context of Bank Main Street, consumers would say, "They're a terrible company. They caused the financial crisis! *They're* going to try to promote home equity loans right now when people are being foreclosed on?"

The bank was getting really, really frustrated by all of this. They kept dismissing our data, saying, "We bought that bank. Those weren't *our* sales practices. We didn't know this was happening, and now we're saving all these people. We're the good guys in this story."

In the focus groups, people would say, "They're not the good guys. I don't care who's bought who or who was there when. You own them, you've got to make this right."

When we shared that data, the bank would say, "But don't they know all the good we do for our communities? We have cultural initiatives, free museum admissions, free baseball games. We support boys and girls clubs and community redevelopment. There is so much that we do."

So we brought that directly to the customers and they responded, "Are you *kidding* me? They took bailout money. They took federal bailout money and their big aha is that they're going to send people to museums?!"

Sometimes our client would actually be behind a two-way mirror, watching this in real time. They'd pass us notes: "Correct that person. Tell them that we already paid back the bailout money. In fact, we were the first company to pay back the bailout money and tell them . . ."

People responded, "I don't care. It's still their fault."

But our clients would continuously try to get us to correct them. Have you ever been in a fight like that? Where someone who has hurt you keeps trying to tell you that you shouldn't feel how you do?

It's not effective.

It got to the point that their reputation was at an all-time low, lower than that of any of their competitors. And they still weren't taking our advice. Then, to make matters worse, in the midst of this crisis they decided that because of the economic environment, they needed to find a way to increase revenue, so they made an announcement that they were going to, down the road, start charging customers a fee for something that used to be free.

It blew up.

The executives had us write a number of different messages on how you talk about the fee. They would say things like "Our customers told us that they want more transparency from the bank. In the most transparent move in the history of financial services, we're telling you months in advance that you're going to pay a new fee. And there are lots of ways to avoid the fee. That's plenty of time for you to figure out how you can get around paying this fee."

We made videos of the responses. One of the participants said, "Okay, wait a minute. So basically you're punching me in the face and I've got a bag over my head. You're gonna take the bag off my head and continue to punch me in the face and I'm supposed to thank you for it?"

Ultimately, the executives made the decision to roll back the fee, but at this point everybody was so fired up, it was as if it had already happened. Occupy Wall Street was camped out all around their headquarters.

Finally the CEO of one of their divisions, and his top three hundred executives under him, brought us in to do a training where we actually showed the video of "So you punch me in the face," and we said, "We understand that you see yourselves as a consumer-oriented organization, but that isn't how you're perceived, and until you address these things, no one is ever going to believe you." It had a huge impact. People still talk about it to this day.

It was at that point that they were finally ready to be vulnerable. They said, "We know it's bigger than just setting the record straight. We need to rebuild our reputation and our brand. What should we say? And how should we do it?" So they engaged us in a project that at the time was very much outside of what we typically had done for them, but now we do for many of our clients: crisis communications.

We'll discuss crisis communications more in depth in chapter 10, but when customers feel violated—and in this case they very much did—trust needs to be earned back. We told them, "You're going to have to really address trust in a way that feels authentic to your customer."

In order to be perceived as authentic, they needed to meet the customer where the customer was, not try to deny their perception. The new language was "There are a lot of factors that led to the financial collapse in 2008. We're not here to debate them, but what we are here to do is show you that we're committed to our customers and the American economy." If they didn't address that the good they were doing was focused on rebuilding the American economy, it wasn't going to make sense to their customer. "We're focused on the fundamentals: building a secure balance sheet, managing our risks appropriately, and most important, making customer-driven decisions."

Once reluctant to talk about the actions they took that directly addressed the financial crisis, they realized the only way forward was to acknowledge that pain point. So they talked about the programs that paid off mortgages or reduced them so that people could stay in their homes. They went to some of the hardest-hit areas and set up pop-up offices to help people navigate bankruptcy and foreclosures so that they could stay in their homes. If the customers couldn't possibly stay in their homes, the bank would help them find other places to live.

That vulnerability had a huge impact. It led them into a much better place, with a new brand, greater market share, and a fully rehabilitated reputation ten years later.

THE HERD MENTALITY

The first clue that you're not being authentic is if you're trying to be like someone else. This is the exact advice your parents gave you in fourth grade, and it's no less true now. At least once a month a financial services company comes to me and says, "We want to be like Apple." And I have to tell them, "No, you don't want to be like Apple. I have data tested this. People do *not* want their bank to be cool. They want their bank to be dependable, established, and responsible. Because technology fails. Phones freeze in the cold and overheat in the sun. Nobody wants the person holding their money to short-circuit or need an upgrade." We have to persuade them that trying to be perceived as "cool" would be counterproductive to every part of their mission. They need to own what they might think of as short-comings, like stodginess, and present these to their consumers as authentic to what makes a bank trustworthy.

Similarly, many brands are obsessed now with persuading consumers that they're "innovative." Internally, every company is focused on innovation. Watch any business show. People are talking about how they "innovate" because Wall Street likes the word and it drives share prices, so they want to lead with it. But when they come in to discuss persuading consumers, it's my job to explain that innovation isn't always a good thing. Sometimes people just want you to serve a function.

One of our clients was a food company that wanted to talk about innovations in the food business. Innovative new menu items, innovative new ways of making your food, innovative new ways of distributing it. But *innovation* is not a word that people want associated with anything they're eating.

In their annual report and press release they put pictures of people in lab coats developing products like fruit juice. But you don't want to see lab coats in your juice—you want to see oranges in your orange juice. So if the goal was to be seen as a great food company, a company of the future that understands diet and health trends for the future, that's fine. But don't be innovative.

Likewise, we had a client who was bringing a new sleep aid to market. They wanted to talk about it being the most innovative sleep aid ever. But our data confirmed really quickly that people don't want an innovative sleep aid, they want a *proven* sleep aid. The problem with sleep aids is that everybody knows that there are trade-offs. The belief in our focus groups was "If I take one, I might get some sleep, but I'm still gonna feel awful tomorrow." What we also learned is that sleep aids aren't necessarily taken because people are anxious about their sleep; what they're anxious about is how they're going to feel *and perform* the next day.

So we told them that instead of saying "innovative," say, "It's a sleep aid without the trade-offs." Because that addresses the pain point or the truth of the person who's using it. You always want to meet consumers at their truth.

SITTING WITH FEEDBACK

This is something that typically makes us uncomfortable; thus it is something we don't often do. It's one thing to say, "I want a promotion within the organization," or "I want to run for local office." Or "I want a raise." It's another thing entirely to ask yourself, *Where do I sit now?* By that I mean: How do people perceive you right now? What are your weaknesses? What are the things that are keeping you from going where you want to go?

I highly encourage people who might not have a formal review process coming up to send out anonymous online surveys. Get feedback on your idea, your proposal, your plan, your performance. Because for persuasion to be successful, you have to meet your audience where they are. That means acknowledging their initial estimation of you, warts and all. *Then* you can shift it.

Here is what this looks like in practice. This is a personal example, from my own 360-degree review a few years ago, but this process is applicable to all feedback. When I started at my company, after all I had done to get there, I was 100 percent committed to my job, and my goal was to grow into a leadership role. But when I sat down to read the assessments, it was jarring how little I had understood of what people really thought of me.

First, people already perceived me as a leader, and I didn't know that. But hold the applause, because they perceived me as a bad leader, one who was trying to be friends with them.

Second, people thought I was a slacker. Because I'd been coming in late frequently.

Third, people didn't think I was a good presenter or thought leader.

Fourth, and this was excruciating, people thought I was driving business by using my looks. And other nefarious activities. Which was *completely* untrue.

Of course, as soon as I got this feedback, part of me wanted to run away, just shut down and find another job. When I tried to imagine changing people's perceptions, I thought I'd never be able to do it.

Then I realized I *had* to. Doing this work was the dream of a lifetime. Moreover, I couldn't coach clients through addressing these same crises and then balk at doing it for myself. So I asked myself, *How do I turn this around?*

I knew I had to do *exactly* what I advised clients: get real about all the misperceptions; validate them, not deny them; and be open. It made me hugely vulnerable. And uncomfortable. I had to make an announcement to our staff that I got their feedback and that I felt it was devastating, but that I had heard it. I said, "I'm committed to doing better. I know it's going to take a while to earn back the trust, but here's what I'm going to do. First, I need you all to know I had surgery six months ago and have been struggling with complications ever since. I should have talked about it. Frankly, I didn't because it was fertility related, which was emotionally really hard, and I wanted work to be a place where I could get my mind off that. But it was a mistake, because of course you wondered where I was. Moving forward, I will mark all my doctor appointments on my calendar and you'll know the exact pockets I'll be unreachable."

So that addressed one of their concerns. We say all the time in our business that anything that is ambiguous will be used against you. It will be interpreted negatively, no matter what. Human beings fill in blanks with negative assumptions. We don't instinctively give people the benefit of the doubt.

To address another of their concerns, I realized that I needed to consciously create fun for employees but then bolt before it got to be friend hour. A leader knows the difference.

Then in the meeting I went on to address what people thought about how I brought in business. I said, "I know I've brought in more business than anybody else this year. Yes, I have a lot of middle-aged male clients that hit on me in front of you [remember, this was in the years before the #MeToo movement], my team members, which makes me incredibly uncomfortable. Frankly, I hate it. It's demeaning and degrading, and the way that I dealt with that was by making a joke out of it. So then everybody made a joke out of it. That was a mistake. Honestly, I struggle with it," I admitted, "and I need your help. I'm not going to make a joke out of it anymore. I'm going to ask you not to make the jokes either."

What ended up happening was a reset. But I achieved that not by saying, "You're crazy! I would never do that!" or "I can't believe you're so hung up on my coming in late when I stay later than anybody!" Right? I could have gotten defensive.

Instead I validated their perceptions, essentially saying, "I am looking at myself through your eyes and see how you came to these conclusions." Once I did that, I could share my side and let them know what would change moving forward and convince them that I was committed to the right things.

RESPECT YOUR WEAKNESS

Recently, a friend's daughter started college, and when she arrived, she thought she wanted to rush the sorority that was known for having the prettiest, most popular girls. But by the end of the week, she realized that she was exhausted. She was working so hard to fit in with their very narrow definition of cool that she was never comfortable with any of them.

I told her she should ask herself, *Who am I, really? Where am I going to thrive?* because it would be where she was having the best interaction with her audience, even if that audience was just the other women at the sorority.

So she picked one where the girls were fun and easygoing and rush was friendly and welcoming. There she felt she could be her authentic self. She is having a great time.

The other night I was on a panel at a women's event. We were asked, "How do you network? Give these women one piece of advice about what they should go out and do." Several socially acceptable answers came to me, but I answered, "You know what, I hate networking. I think the most important thing you can do, if you hate networking, is acknowledge that you hate networking. Because for me, I am incredibly uncomfortable with people I don't know. The way I have overcome this is that instead of working the room, I set a specific goal. If I have two meaningful conversations, then I'm done and can go home.

"I am not saying, 'Don't network.' What I am saying is that you will do it better if you acknowledge that you don't enjoy it and then set attainable goals within that real constraint and hold yourself to them. If you have two or three meaningful conversations, it's still completely productive and you've stayed true to who you are.

"The benefit of this is that you will attend more events if you find a manageable and authentic way to navigate them. You will ultimately network *more* than if you kept trying to pretend this is something you love—and either avoid them or arrive without a plan and hide in the bathroom."

Part of this conversation about limitations is going to be using them to set boundaries and goals. Then hold yourself to something that is reasonable and attainable and will continue to give you a sense of self-confidence.

Because if you sit here and think, *I've got to learn to love networking,* or *I have to join this sorority because everyone is telling me this is the best one,* or *We should do all our brochures in high-gloss white with an Avenir font because it works for Apple,* it's not authentic. Ultimately you won't persuade people to take your card, support your membership, or keep your brochure if it feels like you're trying to be something you're not.

Right now we're living in a world where people like *small batch.* Where people like *craft.* They want their food and drinks to be local, organic, and artisanal. These buzzwords are the opposite of innovative. People want to be as close to their food and the ingredients they put in their body as possible.

Which put our beverage client at an incredible disadvantage. Because they owned a vodka that was suddenly getting pushed out of its market share by Tito's. Now, in their portfolio, that vodka had been their exclusive brand, so they were really flummoxed.

Their first step was to bring in a new branding executive with the assignment of rebranding it as a craft vodka. But she did not think that was a good idea because it wasn't authentic. She came to us to do the market research on that approach and get our input on the direction she wanted to go in, repositioning the vodka in a way that genuinely was authentic.

So the first thing we tested was how people would feel if we used *craft* to describe that vodka. The response was clear—and negative. As we suspected, their target audience said that it didn't seem true or authentic to the brand and they were very sensitive to people using *craft* inappropriately. They pretty much said that everyone was trying to ride the craft train, but you had to be craft in order to say it.

The other part of the picture is that cocktails were becoming more of an experience. You are using what you drink to actually make a statement about yourself. In some ways, it shows that you have a level of sophistication. Your brand of alcohol is telling your own story. Some people were embarrassed to drink vodka in general because brown spirits were more in. So what did that mean for our beverage company?

Well, let's go back to what *craft* means and why people like craft. It's partly because they think craft has a story behind it. It means quality and some level of authenticity. So how then—instead of trying to "be" craft—could this vodka bring out its heritage story? Make the longevity of the brand and the origin of the brand matter.

What we collaborated with her on was reminding consumers about why they ordered it in the first place. In certain parts of the world, having a consistent taste and flavor is as important as anything else. So what this vodka could stand out on was their process and their ingredients. They were one of the first high-end brands, and when we talked about the quality of their process, and the story of how they were the first premium vodka, people responded very positively.

The bottom line: Don't try to blend in. What you need to do is be uniquely you by telling *your* story.

If you're a person who is in charge of making these decisions at your business, don't try to match your brand to a trend that's outside your lane. A few years ago, Coors launched a line of sparkling water when they saw that bottled water was becoming a trend and people were drinking less of their beer. But people don't want sparkling water from Coors. Seeing Coors on the label made consumers feel less good about making the healthier choice. Don't chase the water drinkers if you're a beer company. Be the best beer brand you can be.

If the plan you're proposing is going to cost more, don't hope that no one notices; acknowledge it, then make a case for why it will save money in the long run. If you've never been on the PTA before, make a case for why bringing an outsider's perspective will be advantageous. If your company isn't sexy, say, "We're not sexy, because you don't want sexy, you want reliable." Own the truth of who you are. Because when you acknowledge a truth your client can plainly see, you are instantly engaging in a dialogue with them. You're saying, "I validate and respect your perspective of me. Now let's talk."

PRIORITIZE

When you think about all the stories that I just told, we've identified a lot of weaknesses and then a lot of ways to turn them on their heads, into strengths. So how do you prioritize which ones matter the most to your audience? If you go back to my example about myself when I was trying to work through the 360-degree feedback, there were four areas of concern that needed addressing. To figure out which to prioritize, I used Maslow's hierarchy of needs.

Maslow's hierarchy of needs is a psychological theory put forward by Abraham Maslow in his 1943 paper, "A Theory of Human Motivation." In it, he wrote that people will strive to address their

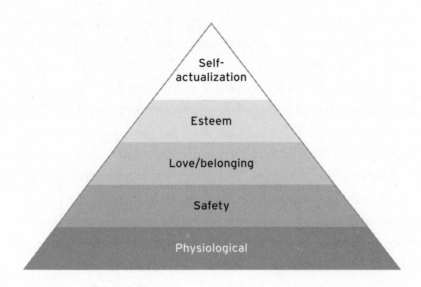

basic needs first. At the bottom we have food, water, and shelter because we cannot survive without those. Then above these, we have safety. Once those needs have been addressed we strive for love and belonging. Then esteem and, ultimately, self-actualization. But if the needs at the lower layers are not being met, the higher levels become irrelevant.

Where this is useful for us is that if a brand has violated the trust of its customers, as was the case with how people perceived Bank Main Street, the company needed to look at which level the violation happened on. The customers they wanted to persuade believed that Bank Main Street had taken away some people's shelter. That is the most basic need. That is a deep violation.

I had to look at my 360-degree review and the four points and ask myself, *Which one violates the deepest layer?* That one was the most important. If I didn't fix that one, I couldn't talk about the rest.

In terms of community contribution, which makes everyone feel safe and secure, I had to ensure that they saw me as a hard worker, as reliable; that they could count on me. Because if people didn't think I was a hard worker, then of course they were going to believe that I used my looks for new business.

If you go back to the Bank Main Street example, they had to ask, "Okay, which need do we address before any of the others?" The bottom line is, if people don't think you've got the fundamentals of banking right, which goes to the heart of people's sense of security, you don't have permission to talk about anything else. That's why they had to go back to basics, emphasizing balance sheets and practices in place to protect consumers. Not free museum visits. Those are at the top of the pyramid.

Remember, you're not prioritizing what *you* think might be the sexiest. Most likely you won't get to talk about the sexiest thing until you've dealt with the other things. For example, when Microsoft launched Windows 7 after Vista, they wanted to talk about how they spent three years innovating and creating all these bells and whistles and that little talking paper clip that would give you tips.

Our focus groups said, "Hold up! I just want to know that it works. Because Vista sucked so badly that I don't even want to use Microsoft anymore. If you innovated on a platform that sucked, you're going to make it worse." That's not what Microsoft wanted to hear. They wanted to talk about innovation, because that's what's cool to them.

But when you are earning back people's trust, you can't start with cool. Once they realized they needed to respect their audience's need for reliability, they went with the slogan "It's Microsoft and it's my idea," which showed leaders in their respective fields using the platform to make things that consistently worked.

When you're prioritizing which vulnerability to authentically address, it's not about the sexiest—it's about what's most important to the people you're trying to persuade.

MAKING THE FLIP

So now that you have a sense of your perceived weaknesses, I want you to think right away about how you can turn those vulnerabilities on their head. If you don't bring the most experience, do you bring the right experience? And a passion that is going to drive you to do all you can for your prospective employer? At the heart of it all, it is our imperfections that make us worth rooting for.

So now I want you to write down those weaknesses. Think about them. How can you turn them into strengths?

Here are a few examples that might inspire you.

Weakness	Flip
We are a small firm competing against larger companies.	We are a boutique firm that is small enough to give you personalized service. You will know each of us personally.
We have no experience working in financial services.	We bring an outside perspective.
We are a large company that is perceived as greedy.	We are large—but we have enough scale to have an impact.
I've made mistakes.	I've made mistakes in the past. And I've learned from them. I've learned to listen more and talk less, to give credit where credit is due, and that sometimes the best answer is *I don't know*.

Weakness	Flip
We violated our customers' trust.	We recognize that we have to earn back your trust. So our commitment to you is *x, y, z.*
You have to give yourself an injection instead of taking a pill.	One injection will keep your medication level stable for an entire week, eliminating your need to remember to take a daily medication.
We use artificial sweeteners.	We use no sugar.
I'm wealthy and out of touch.	I realized the American dream and can help you do the same.
I'm not the best at *x, y, z.*	I'm a fast learner. I can watch anything twice and know how to do it.
I'm a Democrat whom you perceive as elitist and out of touch.	I'm a Democrat raised in a Republican district with Republican parents. I was the first in my family to go to college. I get the struggles. They are real. And I have some real solutions that will help us *all.*

CONCLUSION

If you think about times you've been persuaded, it's most likely because you've been let in on something you never knew before. The center of persuasion is showing something a little bit unexpected. It's not about showing the perfect shiny object.

PART 2

THEM

3

PERSUASION BEGINS WITH EMPATHY

The book *Flatland* by Edwin Abbott made me realize at a really young age that the world looks completely different from different people's perspectives. I'm not sure there's a better lesson out there.

—IAN BREMMER, PRESIDENT AND FOUNDER OF EURASIA GROUP

When you are in a place on an issue where you can't *imagine* why somebody would disagree with you or you find yourself saying, "How could they?" you have an empathy gap. It happens with all the big hot-button issues. People who support climate change legislation think, *How can somebody be so* stupid *as to be a denier? There is science behind it!* Gun control. Abortion. What we are missing from these conversations is empathy. Listening. And respect.

Clients frequently ask me how I'm able to stay so calm and curious in the face of people whose beliefs oppose mine. Let me be clear: to be empathetic, you don't need to agree with people. The digital creator Dylan Marron has racked up millions of views for projects like *Every Single Word* and *Sitting in Bathrooms with Trans People*, but he's found that the shadow of online success is internet hate. Over time, he's developed an unexpected coping mechanism: calling the people who leave him insensitive comments and asking a simple question: "Why did you write that?" He has a podcast and gives a TED Talk on this topic—and I highly recommend you watch it. In it, he explains how sometimes the most disruptive thing you can do is actually speak *with* people you disagree with, not simply *at* them. He says, "Empathy is not endorsement. Empathizing with someone you profoundly disagree with does not suddenly compromise your own deeply held beliefs and endorse theirs. . . . It just means acknowledging the humanity of someone who was raised to think differently."

As far back as I can remember, I have always lived under the assumption that people, even those I disagree with, have good reasons for what they do. The only way that I've ever been able to engage in a conversation with anyone is by trying to come from that place. I might not agree with someone's position, but at least if I understand it, I can begin to engage. As we know from our fractured political climate, most people begin with judgment instead of a willingness to understand. If it isn't flat-out judgment, it is assumptions. Or bringing every experience they've had to the table, instead of saying, there's got to be something there that I'm not thinking about.

Dr. Brené Brown, whom I mentioned in the discussion about vulnerability, encourages readers of her book *Daring Greatly* to make the shift to believing that everyone is doing the best they can with the tools they have. That ultimately it isn't about whether they are or aren't but about how simply *believing* that and approaching every encounter from that perspective will change you fundamentally as a person. Because that is radical empathy.

While not every Persuasion Plan is going to be trying to engage with people we completely disagree with, the lesson still applies, because for the most part we are trying to engage with people who hold a different perspective. When we dismiss opposing viewpoints out of hand, we miss the opportunity for connection, and we render persuasion impossible.

In this chapter we're going to hear from experts in the areas of empathy, neuroscience, and communication to learn how to get to know your audience, your customer, intimately and respectfully. Affectionately, even. Then I am going to walk you through what I have termed *active empathy*, a practice that you can use to reach and persuade in a way that's incredibly effective, because no matter what you are trying to accomplish, everything begins and ends with the audience.

You can't serve your audience until you fully understand who they are and how they want to be served, and the brands that have mastered persuasion—like Nike, Apple, and Starbucks—are the ones that understand that service mind-set.

WHO ARE THEY?

Before you even open your mouth, it's imperative to get clear on this: Who is your audience? That might seem like an obvious step, but I cannot tell you how often I see and hear advertisements, direct mail campaigns, earnings calls, and other forms of communication that are focused simply on what the company wants to say—really just pushing a message—rather than meaningfully engaging and connecting with their target audience.

We must remember: our target audience is the key to our success or failure. Without them, we are nothing. If our message doesn't resonate with them—even if we have the best product, the best résumé, the best action plan, the right policy position, the cutest dating profile—it lands flat. Speaking to your target audience—and by audience, I mean whomever it is you need to persuade, be it the city council or your in-laws—in a way that truly resonates makes you matter. Know your customer—without judgment, without snark.

> This is the golden rule of communicating: Talk to your audience as they are, not as you want them to be.

One of the greatest recent brand strategies to come out of this kind of intimate knowledge was Dove's. Industry colleagues tell me that in 2004, Dove was actually about to shut down the brand, based on weak sales and the executives' perception that the brand wasn't sexy enough. They sent their researchers out to find out how they could "make Dove sexy." Well, after talking with hundreds of women, the researchers came back to say, "You don't."

The research team made the case that the brand needed to be about the *real* beauty of *real* women, authentic, unretouched, and honest. The executive committee responded, "That's crazy. Who does that? No, we're going to close."

The researchers were devastated. They knew their data was right. They knew the strategy they were offering was right. They also knew they had gotten one thing very, very wrong. They hadn't told their story in a way that would resonate with the executive team. They had failed to have empathy with the decision-makers. So they went back to the committee and asked if they could talk to members of the committee's families. After doing this, the researchers brought the executive committee back into the room and showed them a video of the women in their own lives—their daughters, wives, mothers, and girlfriends—talking about how much they hated their appearance, sharing all their insecurities and fears about their bodies, faces, and hair. And this time the men got it.

The brand went back and started truly listening to their customers about their weight, about aging, about never feeling like they measured up. Then, instead of taking the approach every other product line on the market did—"Oh, we can give you something to solve that"—they told their consumers, "You are perfect just the way you are. We celebrate you. And we've made these products to make you feel like the best version of yourself, flaws and all." It was groundbreaking and turned the company into an industry leader.

At our company, we say that there are two truths: yours and theirs. In persuasion, there is only one truth that matters: theirs. If you aren't speaking to that truth, you aren't engaging with them. And without that engagement, persuasion is impossible.

WHAT IS EMPATHY?

Empathy is a word used to describe a wide range of experiences. For the purposes of this book, I am defining *empathy* as the ability to understand other people's emotions, values, and behaviors. This does not mean you have to agree with their emotions, values, and behaviors, but it does mean that you are willing to suspend your own judgment long enough to be able to see the world from their perspective.

Active empathy, which I will teach you here, is a three-step process that covers:

1. **Emotion:** What emotions will make it possible or impossible for me to effectively communicate with my audience?

How can I address our respective emotional states so that we can have a constructive conversation?

2. **Values:** How can I better understand the values that are most important to my audience so that I can communicate about what matters to me in language that resonates with them?

3. **Behaviors:** How can I better understand my audience by looking at what they actually do in addition to what I think they do or what they say they do?

And while each component isn't necessarily new, when people practice empathy they usually focus on only one of the three. What is important here is to go through all three as a unit. I will take you through each dimension and then through how to consciously put it into practice as you get to know your target audience. You will notice some overlap among the three types—that's intentional; how you feel, what drives you, and how you behave are all interrelated. But if you look at these components one by one in a disciplined manner, you will emerge with a full view of your target audience.

HOW DOES EMPATHY WORK?

In order to understand why empathy is so important, I want to start by breaking down how it functions in the body. The word *empathy* itself is derived from the German word *einfühlung,* which means "feeling into." There is a lot of science behind the study of empathy, and more is being added every day. In fact, only in the last ten years have we begun to identify the parts of the brain that control empathy.

Tim Urmston, the CEO of SEEK, is an empathy expert in the corporate world. He simplifies the biology behind empathy with three words: "head, heart, and gut." When you see or hear information, your medial prefrontal cortex takes in the data and comes up with a response strategy. But that action uses only 5 percent of your problem-solving mechanism because there's nothing emotional driving the data further through your system.

Tim explains, "To employ empathy, I want the information to drop to my heart, which is part of my autonomic nervous system. This is also where mirror neurons live." Mirror neurons are responsible for the fear reaction we have when we are simply *watching* someone do something dangerous or scary—jump off a cliff or ride a roller coaster. Whether it's screaming at horror movies or sobbing as we watch YouTube videos of vets returning home, these are the neurons that enable us to live vicariously.

The third level of empathetic connection happens in the enteric nervous system, your gut brain. Scientists are now saying that 95 percent of the serotonin in your body is produced in the microbiome of your gut. The term *gut feeling* has a basis in reality. Tim continues: "So empathy is not only that I know what you know and I feel what you feel, but *because* I'm able to feel what you feel, I'm compelled to act on your behalf. Once I'm able to practice cognitive empathy, the *choice* to connect with someone and allow what they're going through to permeate me, innovation in messaging becomes very interesting and compelling."

TRAINING OUR BRAINS TO BE EMPATHETIC

Our tagline at maslansky + partners is "It's not what you say, it's what they hear."® Understanding what other people hear takes both empathy and discipline. So, I sat down with Dr. Jenny Susser, a certified mental performance consultant with the Association for Applied Sport Psychology and the Team USA Registry, the highest distinction for sport psychology in the United States, to help me understand how we can master empathy as a discipline. She emphasizes that we can use curiosity as a tool to stay empathetic. "Humans are the only species with three full layers to our brains. You can't be curious and emotional simultaneously because blood goes to only one place at a time." The middle part of the brain, or limbic system, controls this flow. When the environment is nonthreatening, blood can fill your frontal lobe, the part of your brain that controls abstract thinking, decision-making, and executive functioning. "But once you become emotional, be it because you saw a saber-toothed tiger or an email with all caps in the subject line, the response in the brain is the same: threat, I'm out." The blood goes south, down to where you are kicking into survival.

In order to override that triggering and have an unemotional, empathetic dialogue, you have to *commit* to wanting to do that. To stay calm as you're trying to persuade, you must stay *curious*.

Jenny says, "A helpful tool is to continuously ask relevant questions like: Where is this person coming from? What happened to them today? Why do they think this way? What is underneath their feelings?" These questions serve two purposes: they increase perspective *and* blood flow to the prefrontal cortex. "When I get in these situations I also ask myself, *Am I arguing, or am I communicating?* Even just asking the question, even if it's not out loud, even if it's not answered, has enough power to bring blood flow back."

EMOTIONAL EMPATHY: THE CHANGE TRIANGLE

Emotional empathy is understanding not only the emotions of the other but the *why* behind those emotions. In order to learn more about this, I met with psychotherapist Hilary Jacobs Hendel, author of *It's Not Always Depression*, because I had heard about her work with the Change Triangle. She has created a model that can help us become more in tune with our emotions and productively move through them. Mastering your emotions is incredibly valuable for anyone attempting persuasion in a potentially triggering context. And while she teaches the Change Triangle in terms of personal development, her lessons are equally applicable in terms of persuasion. Hilary explains the Change Triangle this way:

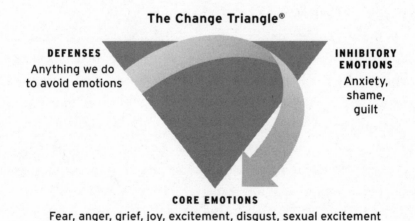

The Change Triangle®

DEFENSES
Anything we do
to avoid emotions

INHIBITORY EMOTIONS
Anxiety,
shame,
guilt

CORE EMOTIONS
Fear, anger, grief, joy, excitement, disgust, sexual excitement

OPENHEARTED STATE of the AUTHENTIC SELF
Calm, curious, connected, compassionate, confident, courageous, clear

"On one corner of the triangle are the core emotions—grief, fear, anger, joy, excitement, sexual excitement, and disgust—the ones hardwired in the middle of our brains and not subject to conscious control. Triggered by the environment, each core emotion sets off a host of physiological reactions that prime us for action." She emphasizes that all of these emotions are *productive,* they give us cues to action, and we shouldn't run from them.

"Then on the next corner are the inhibitory emotions—shame, anxiety, and guilt—which block core emotions and do not serve us biologically. In fact, they keep us from experiencing the emotions we need to in order to serve our purpose."

Where this is applicable to what we are discussing is that your audience must be feeling *productive* core emotions to be persuadable. It doesn't have to be joy. Get people afraid, angry, or disgusted and you can reach them. But if your target audience is feeling shame or anxiety or guilt, they won't be in a persuadable place.

On the last corner are the defenses, anything we do to avoid feeling core or inhibitory emotions: joking, sarcasm, criticizing, spacing out, procrastination, preoccupation, negative thinking, misguided aggression, overworking, overexercising, overeating, undereating, cutting, sex, obsession, addiction, spending too much time on your phone or social media. Hilary continues, "These are the very things we do to avoid engaging in a tough conversation, debate, or even developing a communication strategy."

The Change Triangle works by helping you return to your core emotions as quickly as possible. When an event or situation causes you or your target audience to be off-balance, you must first determine where you or they are on the Change Triangle: defense, inhibitory, or core. Then move clockwise around the Change Triangle until you get to core emotions, which inherently provide guidance to peace, perspective, or solution.

When you are in touch with your core emotions, it leads to what Hilary calls the four Cs: calm, curious, confident, and compassionate. All of these Cs are exactly what is needed to engage in persuasion. I know if I am not in a place where I am feeling any of these Cs, I am not likely to be persuasive at all.

Talking with people who don't share your viewpoint, whether personally, politically, or even at work, will bring up a lot of core emotions. But if we can get you to stay in touch with them—instead of what masks them—you can work *with* them to actively continue to choose empathy.

However, if you go into persuasion from your defensive corner of the triangle—that is, if you're anxious, shut down, or judgmental, or you're practicing avoidance (picture motoring your way through the leftover pie on Thanksgiving rather than having a conversation with your brother that you've been putting off)—it's doubtful persuasion will be successful.

Hilary says, "So much of this is just about awareness. Understanding where you are and what you're bringing in the room. If the person you're trying to persuade gets triggered and you get triggered, the dialogue won't be productive. But if you can stay present and aware of what is happening in your body and project calm, then the conversation can stay on track."

You can use the Change Triangle to evaluate yourself before you persuade as a means of preparation. You can spend time listing all the feelings you have about engaging in the conversation, debate, or marketing plan. How do you really feel about your target audience, your product, or your position? If you find that you are having inhibitory feelings or your defenses are going up, you need to work through them before you engage. If, on the other hand, you are feeling core emotions and are open-minded, you are ready to begin.

You can also use the Change Triangle to understand the feelings of the person or people you are trying to persuade. Working to understand their feelings in response to your issue, position, product, or company is going to be critical to your Persuasion Plan's success.

We worked with a client who managed 401(k) plans. They couldn't understand why every person doesn't invest in their 401(k). To them, it makes sense. Every year you don't save, it's harder to make up for later in life. Once you start doing it, you won't even notice a change in your paycheck. Their arguments were all logical. And that is what they wanted to talk about with their clients. When we asked them what they thought about the people who didn't contribute every year, their response was "These people are misinformed. How could they possibly want to miss out on the opportunity?" So then we asked them, "How do you feel about talking to misinformed people?" They felt anxious about it. Anxiety is an inhibitory emotion that keeps people from being curious and thus from getting to the right answer.

Then we talked to people about how they felt having money come out of every paycheck. They said, "First, retirement is a *looong* ways away. Mortgage payments, bills, childcare, and so forth come every week. So how can we possibly afford to save another dollar?" They avoided opening their 401(k) statement, ignored emails offering incentives, and were so anxious about their future that they couldn't even think about it. All they could think about was today.

Without empathy, what happened? The financial company sent out a list of facts about why you should invest now. And the participants kept deleting the emails and throwing away their envelopes. No persuasion was happening. But once the financial company understood that today was more important to participants than tomorrow— that's when they could build a Persuasion Plan that could help employees invest more of their money without sacrificing the things they needed to get done today.

EMOTIONAL EMPATHY IN PRACTICE

Emotional empathy requires you to be in touch with both your feelings *and* the feelings of the person or group of people you are engaging with. It will require you to stay curious and open. So here are the three keys to practicing emotional empathy.

KEY 1. GET GROUNDED IN YOUR EMOTIONS
ABOUT YOUR ISSUE, PRODUCT, POSITION, OR COMPANY

First, visualize a specific situation in which you will be engaging with your audience. Then describe how you feel, emotionally and physically; get at every uncomfortable sensation. Are your feelings productive or not? Use the Change Triangle to get at the core emotions. See what behaviors might be signals of avoidance. See what feelings might be barriers to your being curious. Try to work through them until you can be open-minded.

KEY 2. GET GROUNDED IN YOUR MISSION

Both psychologists I interviewed for this book talked about the importance of a clear mission to keep as your anchor. To be successful, you need a specific goal, which is what we worked on in chapter 1. Now memorize your mission and make it your mantra. As you go through the process, continuously ask yourself if your message and behaviors are getting you closer to achieving your mission.

KEY 3. GET GROUNDED IN *THEIR* EMOTIONS

Before you set pen to paper, before you enter into an actual debate, before you create a marketing plan, you must have a conversation with people who have the opinion that you're trying to change. If you are trying to sell a new product, talk to the folks you are selling it to. If you are trying to turn around the reputation of your company after a crisis, talk to those who feel they have been wronged. If you are running for office, go out and talk to voters. If you are trying to persuade somebody about gun control, have a conversation with someone who is very supportive of the Second Amendment.

But let me be clear: This conversation is not about trying to change their minds. The objective of this conversation is just to listen. To understand. And to avoid judgment. According to Hilary, judgment is a defense we jump to when we're uncomfortable. Whatever you think you know and whatever assumptions you're making, try to suspend them.

VALUES-BASED EMPATHY

As social psychologist Jonathan Haidt explains in his book *The Righteous Mind*, all communication is values based. Moral foundations theory, which he developed with Craig Joseph and Jesse Graham, posits that humans have six innate moral foundations: care/harm, fairness/cheating, loyalty/betrayal, authority/subversion, sanctity/degradation, liberty/oppression,

Using yourmorals.org, the website developed by the social psychologists who invented this theory as a guide, I will attempt to break down these values for you a bit more.

- Care/harm: This foundation underlies the virtues of kindness, gentleness, and nurturance. This is the value that is primarily associated with programs like welfare, gun control, universal health care, and entitlements. In companies, this value often comes into play in treatment of employees.

- Fairness/cheating: This foundation plays out in questions of justice, or what we believe is fair or right. The question that you would be looking to answer here is whether a person, group, or company acted unfairly or if one group was treated differently from another. This value often comes up in corporate work.

- Loyalty/betrayal: This foundation evolved from our tribal history and comes into play with patriotism and self-sacrifice. The question that you would be looking to answer here is whether a person's, group's, or company's actions were loyal to their pack.

- Authority/subversion: This foundation plays out in issues of leadership and respect for traditions. The question that you would be looking to answer here is whether a person, group, or company showed a lack of respect for authority, didn't conform to traditions, or caused chaos and disorder.

- Sanctity/degradation: This foundation comes from our core emotion of disgust. The question that you would be looking to answer here is whether a person, group, or company violated standards of decency, did something that was perceived as "disgusting." This value has been at play throughout the #MeToo movement as the treatment of various women by men in power has come to light.

- Liberty/oppression: This foundation is about our shared dislike of those who obstruct and restrict liberty and its motivation toward solidarity. This value is often expressed by libertarians, and the question that you would be looking to answer here is whether a person, group, or company was denied their rights.

In order to understand more about how this works in practice, I interviewed Matt Motyl, the executive director of CivilPolitics.org, which he founded with Jonathan Haidt and Ravi Iyer. In addition, Matt is also the research director at OpenMind and an assistant professor at the University of Illinois at Chicago, where he is a social psychologist. He studies what makes communicating with others who hold different moral, political, or religious views so difficult, and what can be done to improve the quality of intergroup communication. He has done extensive work on moral foundations theory and how it plays out in the political world. He says, "We have informally been calling it the 'talking past effect.' We asked people to read about a viewpoint that differs from theirs or is similar to theirs, but with a controlled, neutral topic. What we're finding is that people couldn't remember the details about the counter-attitudinal arguments, but they were really good at remembering the details of the pro-attitudinal argument. It's the equivalent of kindergartners plugging their ears and just going *la-la-la*."

One of the things he has found in his own personal research is that most folks don't talk to people on the other side very often. When these conversations do happen, we are essentially speaking different languages. In one study he did on same-sex marriage, he looked at the language that both sides used in making their arguments. What he found was that liberals would make their pro-LGBT argument in terms of fairness and equality and harm to individuals. At the same time, conservatives were arguing mostly in terms of sanctity of marriage and maintaining the purity of the institution. If one side is saying this is unfair but the other side doesn't even think about the issue in terms of fairness, they are going to have a really hard time seeing eye to eye because they can't even get the language to match up.

He says, "When having a similar conversation about the environment, we were finding that liberals were the ones that were using this sanctity-based argument, thinking about environmental purity and mother earth. Conservatives, on the other hand, argued in terms of fairness. They would say it's not fair to businesses to restrict building things like the Keystone Pipeline."

What he and his companies are trying to do is help people realize that the other side is not necessarily evil or irrational or ignorant. Instead, they are attempting to get people to think about the reasons why somebody might think differently, the essential skill for persuasion.

Values-based empathy extends beyond the moral and political world of Jonathan Haidt to the everyday world of how customers interact with the companies they do business with. From his work on corporate reputation, Michael Maslansky defines a set of what he calls *negative narratives*. These narratives align with Haidt's foundations but are viewed through a different lens. For example, when consumers are shown news stories about product safety issues, Maslansky's research shows that they will assume that the company "put profits over safety." Based on very limited facts, consumers will draw negative conclusions about companies: companies are hiding something or abusing their power or trying to avoid responsibility. These recurrent narratives can be anticipated. Understanding how consumers are interpreting a situation can help you communicate about what really matters to them.

VALUES-BASED EMPATHY IN PRACTICE

Whether you are in politics or in business, in order to translate your language into your target's language, you must first know what value is most important to you on this issue. And second, you must identify which value is most important to your target audience. If you are fighting for stricter gun control legislation, for example, you are probably focused on keeping people, including you and your children, safe. So your primary value would be care/harm. But what value is most important to the person who supports the Second Amendment? If you cull through their arguments—"You can't take away my guns," "I don't want government to tell me what I can do," "I have a right to bear arms"—you will quickly see that they are concerned primarily with liberty/oppression. Once you understand that, you can begin crafting your arguments around the value that matters most to them, not to you.

If you are trying to rebuild the reputation of your company after a crisis, it is common to get defensive. Instead, you need to understand the primary value you have betrayed. If it is an issue of treatment of employees, you need to address harm/care or the appropriate value.

The reason it is so important that you understand both your primary value as well as that of the person or people you are speaking with is to keep you from getting defensive or saying something like "But it's not about that." If you find yourself in that place, it is a surefire sign that you have lost empathy, because to the person you are trying to persuade, it is *exactly* about that.

When we were trying to persuade our beverage client to tell their vodka's origin story or Bank Main Street to address their audience's sense of betrayal, we had to persuade them using the same empathetic tactic.

Their value could have been fairness: "We're a business, too. We've got to make money to keep paying everyone who works for us and continue to manufacture our product." In order to persuade them, we had to start by respecting their moral value. We said, "You're absolutely right, you are a business, and as such you are absolutely entitled to prioritize your financial needs. *But* you're never going to grow your account and your market share unless you understand how your audience is perceiving you and address their concerns." So we acknowledged and respected their value, fairness, and then put forward their customer's value, caring.

This can be especially challenging for some of our clients in tech. The Silicon Valley community values data. Frequently they have figured out the best way empirically and scientifically to do something, and cannot understand when that data alone isn't enough to persuade users. Driverless cars are a great example. According to the data, such cars will save lives. But most people are afraid of them, and we enjoy driving. By and large we make emotional decisions more often than rational decisions, and respecting that can be a challenge for more scientifically minded brands.

Apple, in contrast, understood that to penetrate into the lives of everyone, tech had to start *feeling* friendlier. For their first iMac they used colors and shapes to superficially transform a product that had previously made most people uncomfortable into a friend.

The personal computer became genuinely personal—if not downright cute. How did they get there? By respecting the fears of their consumers and then working to allay them. If Apple had kept looking at computers through their own eyes, they would have missed that enormous marketing opportunity.

BEHAVIOR-BASED EMPATHY

Behavior-based empathy is all about understanding why people do what they do. Tim Urmston was working with a pharmaceutical company to try to figure out why young moms with type 2 diabetes didn't inject their insulin in the evenings, even though they knew the health outcome would be better if they did. We have also done a lot of work in diabetes, and one of the most heartbreaking things to realize is how little empathy doctors and pharmacists have for people with type 2 diabetes. They can't understand why diabetics don't just lose the weight and exercise more. Tim's team wanted to break through these kinds of preconceived notions to get to the truth. Because of course these patients want to be healthy and available to their children. There had to be something else going on.

So he took a team out in the field to watch these moms come home from work, fetch their kids from practice, and make dinner. After a few hours, the team would ask, "Why didn't you take your medicine?" The answer would be "It's hectic. I forget."

Tim says, "That's an insight. You can run with that insight. I call that a nonempathic insight or a traditional insight. You can go out and innovate all kinds of things for her around reminders, phone apps, a buzzer on the package. Companies will do that. They'll run off with these traditional insights and create off of them."

Instead, what his team did was look at all the data they collected from the mothers, trying to imagine being in their shoes, stopping right in the middle of a hectic evening routine to inject a needle in their arm. What emerged was a different narrative: "Every time I put that needle in my arm, I'm reminded I'm broken. Please don't remind me I'm broken in front of my kids." Which led to innovations around patches, pumps, and extended-life pills. Then they focused on messaging that said, "I'm the hero for taking care of myself." By looking at the situation from the mother's perspective, they were able to persuade her to take the medicine that would prolong her health.

It's about bypassing the rational insight—a phone alarm—and asking yourself, *What is this other person feeling?*

BEHAVIOR-BASED EMPATHY IN PRACTICE

Not all of us have the time or resources to do a full ethnographic study as Tim did. So instead, let me offer you a different tool. For behavior-based empathy, your goal is simple: Learn why your audience does what they do when it comes to your issue, product, or company. In order to do that, find someone in your target group to talk with, then get yourself in the mind-set of a journalist taking down facts without judgment.

Here are a few things Dr. Jenny Susser teaches that you can do to ensure you get the most out of these discussions.

- **Be self-aware.** Especially of any triggers you have. We all process information through the lens of our own experience, and we relate what we hear to something we already know. Unfortunately, when it comes to empathic listening, this means we may jump to conclusions too quickly. We may not allow someone to finish explaining their perspective before we put our own label on what we hear and, as a result, judge their experience. In order to engage in empathic listening, we need to stop listening to our own thoughts and really hear our target. If judgments come to mind, let them go and instead ask *why* questions for deeper understanding—not in a combative way, but with a sincere interest and curiosity. Seek to learn who they really are and why they say what they say.

- **Don't allow their style of communication to sway you.** Don't judge them if they speak with an accent or use a lot of filler words, like *um* or *like*. Don't be put off by boldness or too much energy or deterred by shyness or too little energy. All of these things can get in the way of our truly listening. Often we focus on *how* someone is saying something, rather than on what they are saying. Or we become triggered or bored. Realize that if you're starting to judge the person, it may be because you are reacting to their communication style. Don't get distracted by the small stuff; stay focused on understanding the meaning of what the person is telling you.

- **Stay completely focused.** It takes mental energy and willpower to stay focused. This means you can't multitask. No emails. No phone checks. When in person, face the person and look them in the eye. On the phone, do not have your laptop or any screen in front of you. Also, because the part of the brain that keeps us on task runs on glucose, do not go into the conversation hungry. If you can, record the conversation so you can go back and listen to it again. During the conversation, nothing else matters. If you are speaking with people you already know, pretend you've never talked to them before and it's your job to learn everything you can from them.

- **Ask clarifying questions.** Slow down. Don't jump to conclusions. While we often have hypotheses going into these conversations, we often find that we were wrong. For example, I was doing focus groups with Republicans about why they wanted to cut spending on early childhood education programs. I could have assumed that they just didn't care. That they had no heart. But what I learned was that they very much wanted to give every child an opportunity to succeed, but when they heard the terms *welfare* or *spending*, they automatically shut down. When we changed the language from "Support funding of Head Start, the last existing program from the War on Poverty," to "Support investing in our youth through Head Start, so we can ensure that every child has an opportunity to succeed," we had a totally different result. It wasn't that they were heartless, but that they had seen programs from the War on Poverty fail. They had seen spending to excess. They would rather have provided tools for success. And you know what? We changed the language, and financial support remained despite a GOP-led Congress. So I ask that you spend time asking *why* without jumping to judgment. This truly is the route to change.

The questions to ask:

1. What do you think today about the issue/product/ service?

2. What is your experience with the issue/product/service?

3. Where did you learn about it?

4. Who have you talked to about this issue/product/service in the past?

5. Who influences you in general?

6. Where do you get your information?

7. How will this issue/product/service impact your daily life?

8. What matters to you about this issue/product/service?

9. Are you open and receptive to new ideas? Why or why not?

10. What is your *why* for your position? (While this is the last question, it is likely the most important of all.)

ACTIVE EMPATHY: PULLING IT ALL TOGETHER

Oftentimes we get frustrated with our target audience when they don't understand. When they don't listen. I will tell you what we tell all our clients: if they can't hear you, it's not their fault. It's only once you know your audience as much as you know yourself or your product or your company that you can begin to communicate with them. In a world that is filled with clutter, content, advertising, and noise you have to find a way to break through. Your target audience is just one click, swipe, search, or email away from the information that will speak to them. If you don't meet them where they are, they will find the content that will speak directly to them—and that might not be to your benefit. I can't underscore this point enough: *persuasion is an act of empathy.* It takes total commitment and focus. It takes discipline and energy. But if you do it right, it will be worth it, because once you really understand the other, you will be able to engage and move the needle. So if you take nothing else away from this book, please let the information in this chapter shift how you approach persuasion. I promise, it will be worth the effort.

4

HEARING THE HATERS

A fool takes no pleasure in understanding, but only in expressing personal opinion.   —PROVERBS 18:2

If the previous chapter was about ensuring you are in an empathetic frame of mind when you go to persuade, this one puts that on boil. Because here is where we are going to talk about your detractors, your haters, your trolls. Yet I am still going to ask that you stay in an empathetic frame of mind. In fact, it's *essential* that you do so. We find it easy to have empathy for people who agree with us. But where our culture is failing is around the ability to have empathy for people who hold opposing viewpoints.

This is where it can start to feel personal. This is no less true when I'm giving feedback on a brand to their CEO. Most of the time I'm talking about a product the CEOs didn't invent, one that has been manufactured and distributed by other people, but still they receive the negative feedback as if I have just told them their haircut is awful or their dog is funny looking. It hurts. It *seems* like it would be really easy to ask, "Okay, so what do they think about me to begin with?" but guess what? It's touchier than that, it requires more vulnerability than you'd think, and most people go very wrong here when they get negative feedback.

The important thing to keep in mind is that this is still the same group you were getting to know in chapter 3. You cannot shut down to their opinions and their values just because they don't currently align with your own. Throughout this process we must continue to try to know the other and stay brave.

Emile Bruneau, a cognitive neuroscientist at the University of Pennsylvania, is an expert in empathy and has found that it is much more difficult to have empathy with someone with whom you are inclined to disagree. In "The Brain's Empathy Gap," an article in *The New York Times Magazine,* Bruneau explains, "When considering an enemy, the mind generates an 'empathy gap.' It mutes the empathy signal, and that muting prevents us from putting ourselves in the perceived enemy's shoes." If we do not like the person we are going in to persuade, we are inclined to unconsciously suppress empathetic feelings toward that person. That means we must make a conscious effort to engage in empathy. It doesn't come naturally.

Recently a friend of mine was in a heated disagreement with her seventy-two-year-old father because she wanted to evolve some holiday traditions to be more inclusive of her husband's family, who are of a different faith. Things were getting a little ugly at my friend's house when her eight-year-old daughter stepped in. "Grandpa has one way of doing things and it's not wrong. Daddy has another way of doing things and that's not wrong. You're trying to make everyone happy and that's not wrong. But everyone is different, and everyone is allowed to have different feelings."

They all laughed because the daughter was so completely right. They'd been trying to figure out who was right and who was wrong, which is always a losing proposition, instead of talking with one another about what was important to each of them and why. Once they did that, they found there were some things the grandfather was willing to let go of, which made space for the events the son-in-law valued, and the traditions evolved. In the end everyone felt seen, heard, and respected.

In this chapter I'm going to teach you how to communicate, connect with, and yes, persuade (some of) your haters to change their tune, while still respecting the core of who they are and what makes them different.

We can bridge far more divides in this country than we currently are if we come at them with the goal of connection and bilateral education rather than "I am going to teach this person that he is wrong and I am right." That approach never works. It goes against our neurobiology and deepens conflict.

But please know this: nothing I am going to be suggesting in this section is easy for anyone. Hearing criticism is triggering. Hearing opposing beliefs can be as well. For the sake of the goal you identified in part one, I'm going to ask you not to simply rise above that but to breathe through it. And I'll give you some helpful techniques for staying objective and receptive, even in the face of an attack.

Because persuasion is about fostering connectivity. We must remember that, no matter who is sitting across from us, we all have far more in common than we may think.

A WORD ABOUT CRITICS

Before you even find out where on the spectrum from adulation to condemnation your audience resides, you have to make peace with one thing: you are never going to convince everybody of everything that you want to, and sometimes incremental progress is enough. You have to be realistic about this when you take a close look at your detractors, because you're entering controversial territory. There's risk involved, and with risk comes a downside. Johan Jørgen Holst, who helped negotiate the Oslo Accords, said that the mistake most people make in negotiation is trying to get their audience from *A* to *Z*: "You are just trying to get them from *A* to *B*." It's a game of inches.

The way I explain this to my clients is that if our country hadn't made small steps with gay marriage, there would be no gay marriage. First people in favor started by saying, "We want to make sure that gay people have equal rights," which led to equal protection under the law. Then "We want to give gay people civil unions," which led to that legal evolution. Were it not for those two incremental steps, we wouldn't have gotten to marriage equality, because the perception would have been that there was too much fear. It was a game of inches that led to big things happening.

Of course, it goes without saying that this can be hugely frustrating and patience-testing when you just want to get to your goal already. Especially when you're talking about human rights. People say, "Why should we have to be patient? Why should someone with hate in their heart limit my rights or liberties?" But that, too, is an assumption. When we are talking about persuasion, we have to hold tightly to the belief that *all* opinions can evolve.

Also, just because you're being criticized doesn't mean that you're doing anything wrong. In fact, I would argue that, after all my years in the persuasion business, if you're dealing with somebody who's negative or a hater and you get some backlash, you're probably doing something right. You're taking a stand. And that is the future of communication. Being blandly in the background doesn't work anymore.

TAKING THE BASELINE

The first thing we need to do is figure out how your audience is feeling about you/your proposal/your company/your product *right now*. This needs to be an honest snapshot of where you're starting from so you know exactly how far you have to go.

If you are trying to persuade on a personal scale, you can ask for feedback in an email or in person. But know that your responsibility is to receive that feedback neutrally. You are on a fact-finding mission, so you don't want to jump down anyone's throat or inhibit their honesty. You don't want people to tell you solely what you want to hear, then vote against you when it counts. By the way, I don't use *voting* only in the pure sense of the word. It can apply to your living room or at the next team meeting.

If you're proposing something on a company-wide scale, try using a service like SurveyMonkey to solicit anonymous feedback on your performance or proposal. If you are a company or brand, focus groups are the best way to gather honest data from your target consumer.

Once you have your feedback, the responders will fall into four groups. The first is your fans. We love them, but they don't get any airtime in this chapter. The second category will be people who think nothing of you. They don't know about you, they're not thinking about you, you're not even on their radar. The third group is those who have a negative opinion of you, but it's not necessarily emotional. It's more that they don't think your product or position works, or they think your brand is cheaply made, or that you're not that smart. The fourth group is the most challenging to deal with, but one that is increasing in prevalence: the haters. We have become a society defined as much by our hates as by our loves. A hater is someone who has a deep-seated opinion about you, and this is the person we focus on most in politics. Because there is really no gray anymore. The world is seen as either black or white. You're with me or you're against me, and if you're against me, you must be evil, and therefore I must hate you, right?

This category is reserved for things that are political, spiritual, values-based, or significant to people's lives. On a corporate level, this is a data breach that impacted millions of people and your identity was stolen and it cost you personally. Your neighbor's home was foreclosed on, and therefore you hate the bank that did it. It also covers the most incendiary issues we're facing as a country: abortion, guns, and the environment. But before we cover how to make progress across such deep divides, let's first discuss those who have no opinion and those who have a negative opinion (remember, we're not talking about the fans).

NO OPINION

Companies and people alike are tempted to ignore those whose baseline is having no opinion about us. It's human nature to chase the prodigal son or the one that got away. We get so focused on serving our existing base or quieting our detractors that we often forget that the people with no opinion are ripe for persuasion. So consider talking to those often-dismissed no-opinion people and asking them, "*Why* don't you have any opinion of us? How could we correct that?"

If you send out your survey and the results tell you that most people have no opinion about you or your proposal, that means you have work to do to spread your message—but that is a real opportunity as well. We see this frequently with mutual funds, annuities, and tech companies, industries where people on the inside forget that people on the outside might have way less interest in them than they think. People closest to those products are often shocked to learn that the average person doesn't have a strong opinion on their financial or technology product. Often they would rather focus on the people who are already in the market for that type of product.

While yes, it's important to persuade the people actively looking for that product, it's also important to recruit people who may not even have realized they were in the market to begin with.

But that is the work of parts three and four. We'll get there. In the meantime, we're going to focus on the last two categories because that is where the hard work lies.

NEGATIVE OPINION

Reacting in anger and annoyance will not advance one's ability to persuade.
—RUTH BADER GINSBURG

For the first ten or so years I did this work, it was commonplace to ignore haters and critics entirely. I would do focus groups, and we would start by screening candidates to make sure we got the right people in the room. One of the things that the clients wanted to screen for was their opinion of the product, the company, or the issue. We'd use a 10-point positivity scale, and the general attitude was that anyone who was rating between a 0 and a 3 wasn't worth having in the room because we thought their minds were made up.

So we just wouldn't recruit those folks. But times have changed. In today's social media, and its always-on environment, we can't ignore haters. And we now know we can win them over if we engage them in the right way. Ignoring them entirely is a huge waste of opportunity and one of the key contributing factors leading to what we are now calling the *echo chamber effect* in politics. People are more comfortable hearing from different voices in their own choir than from opposing viewpoints.

The tragedy of this perspective is that once you're elected to any office, you represent *all* your constituents, not just the ones who voted for you, not just the ones who agree with you. So if you never take the time to hear from and understand those who disagree with you, how can you represent their interests? Most likely you won't . . . and our divide deepens.

The other practice that was commonplace was to avoid the risk of doing or saying anything that could be construed as controversial in order to avoid any backlash. We would run focus groups to make sure that the ad the company wanted to run or the campaign they were about to launch wouldn't ruffle any feathers. No one wanted to risk alienating any potential consumer.

The climate today is very different. Brands that don't express a viewpoint, even on issues that have nothing to do with their product, can seem suspect now in the eyes of consumers.

After the mass shooting at Marjory Stoneman Douglas High School in Parkland, Florida, Dick's Sporting Goods made an announcement and took out national ads saying they were going to do their part to support commonsense gun ownership by ceasing the sale of assault-style rifles and raising the minimum purchase age to twenty-one. That never would have happened even just a few years ago because it would have been perceived as too much of a risk to potentially alienate their NRA-member consumer base.

Instead of making a public statement, companies just privately wrote big checks to support their beliefs. In the room, they would go to all the trouble and expense of hiring us to put these focus groups together and then test the most conservative version of their message. Essentially they were saying, "We're launching this new product that you probably already want," and the people in the room would say, "That sounds great, because you already preselected us to be the people who'd probably want it." It was a feedback loop, and nothing brave happened.

Now more than half of Americans think that corporate America is going to make real change in this country, not government, so there is an expectation that companies and leaders are going to take a stand and make the hard decisions. The biggest risk then was actually saying something, and today the biggest risk is saying nothing. According to the 2018 Cone/Porter Novelli Purpose Study, 78 percent of Americans will buy a brand for the first time based solely on the brand's position on a controversial topic. Half of people make purchases based on companies' beliefs or values. Fifty-one percent will be more loyal buyers of a brand that speaks up compared with those that remain silent, and 48 percent will advocate for and defend a brand that speaks up and criticizes the competitors that don't. Thirty percent are buying or boycotting more products than they were in just 2014. All this means that we're in a place where you're going to have to put your neck out, and when you put your neck out, not everybody is going to agree with you.

Up until this point, our instinct in our personal and professional lives has been to say, "We're not going to talk to them, because 'haters gonna hate.'" But if you think about an issue like gun control, whether you're Dick's Sporting Goods or one of the Million Mom Marches, if we don't talk to haters, we're never going to have change, because according to a Quinnipiac poll released in 2018, 97 percent of Americans support requiring background checks for all gun buyers. That means the conversation is being held up by a vocal 3 percent. If we don't persuade lawmakers that they must have the backs of the 97 percent, meaningful change will never happen.

PERSUADING EVEN THE HATERS

In 2017, we did a project for an organization that wanted to shift perceptions about Muslim Americans. Our role was to define language that could facilitate that shift. What was brave was that the organization expressly wanted to hear from haters. So we selected Caucasian Americans who were conservative, who voted for someone besides Hillary Clinton in 2016, who answered questions that revealed prejudice against Muslims in a questionnaire, and none of whom had any personal relationships with Muslim Americans.

What happened next was profoundly humbling. We had the erroneous belief that if these people simply met Muslim Americans, then each group would have some awareness of the other, and it's much harder to hate anyone up close. But it turned out their prejudices were strong and deep-rooted, and the process of just giving them facts—such as 10,000 Muslim Americans are serving in our nation's armed forces today; or that the majority of terrorist attacks on U.S. soil are actually carried out by far-right extremists, not by Muslims; or that Islam was the first religion to give women the right to own and inherit property—was all met with complete disbelief and often outrage.

What we had to do was find a way to dispassionately *understand* their baseline. Their baseline was that they had very strong views on American values, so being American to them meant freedom and patriotism, respecting the flag, respecting our armed forces. We thought that if freedom—specifically, religious freedom—was a value, then why wouldn't they be open to people who came here to enjoy our religious freedoms? But these folks were really afraid that their values were under attack, and the Muslim community was part of what they saw driving this change to American values.

When we said *Muslim American* to this audience and asked them to write down the first words or phrases that came to mind, they wrote down things like *foreigner, immigrant, outsider, terrorist,* and *not like me.* What was worse was that they thought they already knew Islam. They had strong opinions about the nature of Islam, and all of those strong opinions were based on what they knew about terrorists, not on what they knew about Muslims.

When I say you need to understand their baseline, it may mean you need to have somebody other than you engage in the conversation with the people you're trying to persuade. In this case it was helpful that the Muslim American organization had hired us to be their intermediary, to test messaging and ask the necessary questions, while keeping our personal feelings out of it. If we had just gone ahead and put the two groups in a room together, it's unlikely anything productive would have come out of it.

Persuading haters takes intense curiosity, it takes discipline, and sometimes it takes creating some distance, because hate is hard to hear. It was really challenging, but our job as persuaders was to hold in our heads that these people we were interviewing were decent people who simply held beliefs we found prejudiced and hurtful. Think of the first Thanksgiving after the 2016 election. So many people had to go back home to families they loved and respected, whose vote had felt like a gut punch. But they said, "This is my dad," or "This is my mom, this isn't a bad person. How do I connect with them?" Our job was similar.

We tried a number of different approaches. The first we tested was: On the assumption the haters think that Muslim Americans don't share their values, let's have Muslim Americans say that they do. So the Muslim Americans said, "We share the same values as you," and the haters responded, "No, you don't. You have no idea what my values are. You're from another country." Even if the Muslim person speaking was a second- or third-generation American, the haters would still say that. It got worse when we tested Muslim Americans saying, "Many Americans grew up learning lessons in the Bible, like respect for life and the importance of charity. Most Muslim Americans learned the very same lessons, just from a different place: the Quran." Now, we might all go back to the Old Testament, but do not tell these people that the Muslim god is the same as the Christian god is the same as the Jewish god. To them, that is outright offensive; they got so triggered they couldn't listen to us. As we say all the time at the firm, facts don't set you free.

The next thing we tested was having the Muslim Americans say, "There's a small minority of people using our religion to justify horrific acts. We need your help to defeat these terrorists." The response was "You know what? The problem is it's your religion that's gone rogue. You need to deal with it yourself."

Another tactic we tried was saying, "It's time that each of us makes a decision about who we are and what we want to stand for. No American can stay silent in the face of this kind of hate and intolerance," and the haters replied, "Talk about hate or intolerance! Your people are killing our people."

We kept meeting walls. After an excruciating amount of trial and error, what we finally discovered were three tactics that could get through to haters. The first tactic was, instead of talking about shared values, finding something we could all agree on. What did this look like? Well, in this case the first thing was talking about why we're all living here in America. We tested a Muslim American man saying, "The beauty of living in this country is that America offers everyone an opportunity to chase their dreams—the dream of working hard and building a successful life for ourselves in a community founded on freedom and equality." *That* was received very positively.

What's different about that approach is it's actually not saying, "You and I are the same," but it is *demonstrating* the similarity by talking about American values and the American dream we can all agree on.

The second tactic was, instead of giving a hostile audience facts, telling stories and showing the people beneath those labels. Rather than what we did at the beginning, telling them that there are 10,000 Muslim Americans serving in the U.S. armed forces, we talked about *one* man in the military—what he did and what his family was like. Instead of calling themselves Muslim American, we found the response was much better when they led with what they had in common with the people they were trying to persuade, e.g., describing themselves as Americans of Muslim faith, showing that they identified foremost as American. Then they followed up with "Part of me is being Muslim, but I'm also other things, too. I'm an architect, a father, an American, an Eagles fan. Americans of Muslim faith, like me, are all different, but we're all Americans."

The third tactic was the most effective, and that was showing that the Americans of Muslim faith acknowledge and respect their target audience's concerns. They said, "You know, after seeing news stories from across the world, we find it understandable to have concerns about the role of Muslims in America. I want you to know we are speaking out to condemn violence. We are working to have ongoing town halls so we can meet other Americans and answer their questions. We're encouraging our communities to be vigilant about any type of extremism."

This tactic really opened things up, because they were making the hostile audience feel heard. Without that, you're never going to move things forward. This is one of the biggest things that we learned; it seems like you're taking a step backward, but acknowledging the concern of the haters is actually the one way that you move things forward.

Ultimately, of course, one could say, "Wait, it's the Muslim Americans who are on the receiving end of prejudice; they should be the ones *receiving* empathy!" But they are the ones who want to *do* the persuading. So no matter what, to be successful in their attempts they needed to find a way to dig deep and have conversations with the audience that was judging them.

SHEDDING SHAME

When we're trying to persuade haters, we often have an inclination to use shame, especially in politics. But this is 100 percent the wrong tactic because, as we learned from the Change Triangle, *shame shuts people down*. On social media or in the twenty-four-hour news cycle, we frequently hear, "If you vote X way or think X way, you're an idiot." We don't denigrate the opinion, we denigrate the opinion holder. Even when the objective is to persuade someone to shift their thinking. People will reach out to family members across party lines, but say, "Don't you read a newspaper?! Don't be a sucker." Of course the response is "I'm not an idiot. Don't call me an idiot."

No one in the history of the world, when confronted with having believed a false piece of information, has ever said, "Oh my god, you're right. I *am* an idiot. Thank you." That just doesn't work, because the more combative people feel, the more they're going to define themselves by their opposition, essentially digging in their heels.

If Democrats want to make headway with the constituents who feel left behind from the economic recovery, they need to *listen*. A candidate would need to say, "I feel your pain. [Remember that?] I get that you feel government has failed you. That politicians have failed you. I'm here to tell you that starting today it's going to be different. And here are three things I commit to do to grow the economy so you will feel the difference in your bank account." Honesty is disarming.

The most powerful and effective piece of language that we tested was "After seeing news stories from across the world, we find it understandable to have concerns about the role of Muslims in America." The language wasn't defensive. Instead, it validated their audience and met them where they were. It was saying, "We're aware of what the challenge is." Remember, acknowledging isn't the same as endorsing. Finding a space of agreement defuses the hostility because common ground is found.

Finding the disarming entry point is one of the most important tactics when you're dealing with a hater, even though you might not understand them at all. One of my friends is highly visible on Twitter and periodically attracts trolls with her more political posts. She always tweets back, "I respect your position," and they never say anything further. But note she doesn't say, "It may surprise you, but I respect your position," because that would be a little snarky and would imply that they are ill informed. She sticks with a simple "I respect your position, but I also support free speech," or "I respect your position, and also appreciate that Planned Parenthood provides free cancer screening for tens of thousands of women each year."

I will thank haters for letting me know I've offended or upset them. If we keep meeting anger with anger, the world's divisions will only escalate. Persuasion is a communication-based process. If we're all just shouting so loudly that we can't hear the other person, we can't communicate.

A LOW-STAKES PRACTICE

If you'd like to practice this technique without diving right into engaging with your critics, spend some time with children, especially toddlers. Frequently when kids hurt themselves, adults will say, "You're fine," or "That wasn't so bad," and the children get more upset. Instead, try mirroring back to them or validating their perspective: "Wow, that was a big tumble. Did that hurt? It looked ouchie." Watch the tears dry right up.

It's in our hardwiring to need to feel seen and heard. The next time you are with family members who think or vote differently from you, instead of getting angry, try getting curious. Imagine you have been sent to this house to interview your aunt for a portrait of a viewpoint. It's your job to come away not having changed her mind but understanding *why* she thinks what she does.

Then you can go away and think about what she might be able to hear that would both validate her perspective *and* introduce some new information.

A HIGH-STAKES PRACTICE

Recently we did a project where we were tasked with finding the language that would make the biggest possible impact on climate change. Several agencies bid for the account, but ours was the only agency that decided, "You know what? We're actually gonna go out and talk to people who are climate skeptics."

We found people who fit the demographic, which is 30 percent of the population, but more male, older, white, and wealthier. They are more religious, are more likely to be Republican, and live in rural areas. Eighty percent of them believe that the government interferes too much in their lives. Nine out of ten think respect for authorities is something all children need to learn and don't exhibit enough of right now.

When we asked them what they think of when they hear *climate change,* the answers were that prices are going to go higher and there's going to be increased regulation and unequal burdens on countries.

They wanted tangible proof that global warming is man-made.

It would have been very easy at this point to get frustrated, right? But the reason so little progress has been made in this conversation is that the deniers feel talked down to and made fun of. It comes back to that same principle that we just talked about. When was the last time someone changed your mind by saying you were wrong? The alternative? Conversations. Suspending judgment. Maintaining curiosity. Meeting people where they are and finding common ground.

When we did these focus groups, my super curious team was surprised that the more they engaged with deniers, the more they were finding out that "Oh my gosh, the deniers actually do care." The deniers said things like "Yeah, well, the city may pass a plastic bag ban in favor of the environment, but you know what they do? They let developers bulldoze an entire forest so that they can have something new." Other people said things like "God wants us to be good stewards and use resources wisely. I just don't want to be told that I have to do it by the government."

When we were having conversations, we found that these people did care about the environment, so it didn't help the cause to shower them with statistics and tell them things like "You can't ignore the fact that this year we had more flooding than ever before." Instead, we were able to persuade deniers by shifting the focus and finding common ground.

Instead of using the language of the values of the climate change movement, we had to use the language of their values. We didn't have to give them new reasons to care. They already had their own reasons to care. We just needed to celebrate and elevate them. Really it was about reframing the conversation by showing people they could relate to supporting climate change efforts, without making anybody admit that they were wrong.

For the ad campaign we said, "Let's show real people." The text with the photograph read, "My name's Steve. I come from a third-generation coal family. I founded a company that helps coal miners learn solar power panel installation and management skills. It's giving technician credentials and creating jobs right here in West Virginia. I'm doing it for the people who raised me."

Another said, "My name's Bill. I'm a hunter, an elder at my church, and a proud Republican. I also run a nonprofit that protects water quality on the Colorado River and teaches farmers about the impact on the environment. I used to fish here, but now I can't. I'm doing it for the rivers I grew up with."

"I'm Sally. My family has farmed in Central California for over forty years. My husband and my son used to get up every morning at dawn to work. As farmers and Christians, we try our best to be good stewards of our land. Last year we woke up to wildfires destroying half our crops. I'm now sharing my story. I'm doing it for the land we lost."

The campaign didn't focus on silencing deniers or flogging our facts as opposed to your facts; instead it was more about conservation and energy issues, giving pro-conservation conservatives a face. But it was possible for us to get there by having empathy for the deniers.

ACTIVE EMPATHY WITH HATERS IN ACTION

Current hot-button issues for consumers are genetically modified organisms (GMOs), the overemployment of pesticides, and the overuse of antibiotics in dairy. There are haters. There are skeptics. And a recent study showed that people were willing to pay more for a product labeled "*xxx*-free," even when *xxx* was a made-up ingredient.

So when a company who manufactures pesticides came to us to help improve their reputation, we knew it was going to be no small undertaking. How on earth do you convince folks that a company like that is good? It starts with active empathy.

The number one thing when it came to this company specifically is that they were associated with negative practices that people haven't liked about agriculture for a generation now. They made GMOs. They made pesticides and crop protection products. They were seen as a big evil corporation that both enabled and encouraged some of the worst practices in agriculture today. The idea that this company could be helping farmers and helping agriculture and specifically making agriculture more sustainable was a pretty high bar for many people. When we spoke to folks nobody bought it.

We had to find common ground. We found that what mattered to people was that they wanted to feel good about the food they ate and where it came from. We had to find out what this company could say that would meet those needs of the consumer. It sounded like it might be impossible, right? Not at all. In fact, there were a lot of different ways they could talk about what they did that helped their target audience. They could talk about innovations in plant breeding. They could talk about how farmers are increasingly using their data and software to be more precise and reduce waste; they could talk about increasing the use of science to create better crops. They could try to start broadening the conversation beyond GMOs and pesticides.

What we found was that the digital tools this company offered helped shift the conversation. Many farmers liked using their software, smartphone apps, and other digital tools to help them make long-term decisions. Much of the time, science and farming don't seem to go together because it feels like you're changing the food. Whereas offering digital tools is broad enough and can be redefined in such a way that it becomes about how farmers can take advantage of these tools to improve their practices and actually use less of the things that consumers want them to use less of—land, water and resources.

In the end, the client built a campaign around this idea: "Keep Mother Nature's gifts where they belong. Use less water, use less land, use less energy." Here's one story they told: "Imagine if we could grow plants that treat the symptoms of rheumatoid arthritis. Or plants that convert sunlight into food more efficiently. Or bioluminescent plants that glow in the dark, lining a city sidewalk or hiking trails. Seem outlandish? Not to people like Sharon Berberich and Sam Fiorello, who spend nearly all their time imagining the future of plants and agriculture." Then they went on to talk about what the future of technology could do to help farming use less water, land, and energy. Without active empathy, this campaign would never have been possible. They would have gone about convincing folks that they were a great company without understanding what was most important to consumers.

BE PREPARED

It's important you know that when we say, "Don't be afraid to communicate with haters," that doesn't mean the critics won't be vocal. You've got to prepare yourself for the extreme response. What happens if you get trolled? What happens if people come at you and verbally attack you? Or call for a boycott of your products? When Keurig pulled their advertising from Sean Hannity's show, people were breaking their Keurigs, but guess what? Keurig weathered it without caving, and their market share is as strong as ever.

Recently we developed a social strategy for a telecom company that was working to rebuild their reputation after becoming known mostly for dropped calls and spotty service. They wanted to take a stand on cyberbullying because so much of it happens on devices using their broadband. It was holistic and made sense. But they also knew that they were going to get crucified by trolls at the same time, because that's the world we live in now. So we were prepared. When trolls came at them with tweets like, "You know who's a bully? Your billing department!" we had a hundred prepared fun tweets in response, with links sending them to cyberbullying counseling, and the trolls settled down pretty quickly.

When Chick-fil-A announced their stance on gay marriage, it was risky because they're the third most popular fast-food chain in the country. But they were prepared for it. They put signs up in their stores explaining their position as a Christian company. They told their employees what to expect and what to say. They had their CEO announce it by saying, "We don't judge anybody. This is just our belief."

If you know that critics are going to come, but you address them in the right way, it's actually only going to elevate you, not defeat you.

The right way is to know what the criticisms are going to be and handle them without being defensive. Get someone to play devil's advocate and try to think of the worst thing someone might come at you with. List all the potential criticisms you could receive. Is it just you, because you're an individual? Or are you a company that needs to make sure that all your employees are prepared? Do you have a social media presence? Do you have a strategy for how to answer trolls who are going to come at you? Are you doing media interviews? You know you're going to get questions. How are you going to answer them?

Most important, remind yourself of your goal, what you said you were going to do, what you've accomplished, and how much progress you've made so far. Say, "We expected turbulent times, and we understand that we're receiving a lot of criticism, but we're also moving things forward."

Then take the high road, not the combative road.

HEARING THE HATERS

Thus far we have been focused on shifting the thoughts of the haters, but sometimes the haters have some valid points that need to be taken in and it's you who is going to need to pivot. Sometimes it's okay to change your position based on opposition. That doesn't mean that you failed.

Over the years Obama said his position on gay marriage "evolved." He said he had met and listened to his critics and his critics had helped shift his thinking. In 2015 Starbucks tried to launch a campaign called "Race Together." When they got backlash because Caucasian consumers on their way to white-collar jobs, who could afford the product, felt uncomfortable receiving the cups from their baristas of color, who clearly also didn't want to be having a conversation about race while serving coffee, they pulled it. Not every well-intentioned initiative is a winner.

In February 2018 Weight Watchers announced that it would offer free memberships to teens over the summer and there was such an overwhelming backlash from the eating disorder communities that they pulled the program, which also may have been well intentioned but was perceived as "hooking" teens on a program whose financial model is based on recidivism. Rightly or wrongly, the promotion was perceived as more self-interested than altruistic.

ACTIVE EMPATHY IN CONTROVERSY IS UNCOMFORTABLE BUT POSSIBLE

I tell my clients that if I haven't made them uncomfortable during an engagement, I haven't done my job. For the most part, empathy is talked about passively as something that happens naturally with people we care about. What I am urging you to do is get out of your comfort zone and apply active empathy with people you are inclined to disagree with—and even be triggered by. Active empathy means the burden is on you to do something to understand other points of view. As a persuasion tactic, proactively putting yourself in someone else's shoes is a powerful tool that will make the difference between talking at someone and engaging in a dialogue that will change minds. This isn't for the faint of heart. It takes commitment. I promise you, though, if you do it, it will pay off.

PART 3

CONNECTION

5

—————

YOUR THREE PILLARS

You can't build a great building on a weak foundation.
—GORDON B. HINCKLEY

Inevitably within acts of persuasion, there will be times you will get
challenged. You will make your case, only to receive pushback or
contradiction. You'll get emotional or sidetracked. This next part of
the process of persuasion is going to be about building the foundation
of your argument in such a way that no matter what headwinds you
encounter, it can't be blown away. By the end, you will have the tested
points you can make over and over until people remember you and
what you stand for.

The counterintuitive part of this process builds on our work in
part two. Instead of laying a foundation based on you yourself—your
desires and what you think of your product, plan, or proposal—you
are going to build it based on your audience. The foundation must be
empathetic to resonate with them over the long term and ultimately
persuade them.

THE MASTER NARRATIVE

The fact is, the biggest decisions about you are going to be made when you're not in the room. You won't be there when customers make the final call on which product goes in their cart or who the new hire is or whether your email gets read or which name is circled in the voting booth. Which is why you must have a powerful *master narrative*, the thing you want people to say about you when you aren't there.

A master narrative is your singularly focused message that defines and differentiates you. It is a focused idea that lives in all communication about you. It takes different forms and words, but its spirit is always connected. Once you have found it, it becomes your true north, the criterion against which everything else aligns.

Nike's "Just Do It" tagline was an expression of their master narrative of bringing out the athlete in all of us. GE's "We Bring Good Things to Life" was an expression of their master narrative that their diverse products make life good for everyone. Smucker's "Choosy Moms Choose Jif," is an expression of their master narrative of quality ingredients in a quality product for a discerning consumer. Ronald Reagan's "Morning in America" was an expression of his master narrative of renewing American values and promise. These are just some examples of powerful master narratives in our history that go way beyond a slogan or a campaign. They dictated every decision the brand or party made for years and years, sometimes decades, so that everything would always support the narrative. Note that all of these master narratives persuaded by making their audience feel good about themselves. The audience was able to think, "I'm not just buying sneakers, I'm an athlete." "I'm not just buying a lightbulb, I'm supporting progress." "I'm a discerning mom doing the best for my family." "I'm endorsing the dawning of a new day for the country I love." That is why empathy is essential to this process, because until you can truly understand what your audience wants to *feel*, you can't create a master narrative that gives it to them.

In this chapter we're going to focus on how you discover and build the three pillars of your Persuasion Plan, which will each be supported by your proof points, or facts. Below is the visual template we use with clients for the process.

MASTER NARRATIVE

Pillar One	Pillar Two	Pillar Three
Proof Point 1	Proof Point 1	Proof Point 1
Proof Point 2	Proof Point 2	Proof Point 2
Proof Point 3	Proof Point 3	Proof Point 3

Once we have all three pillars and nine proof points, then, in the next chapter, I'm going to give you some examples of master narratives that worked and ones that didn't. Finally, we'll walk through the five steps for you to use to identify your master narrative. At the end of the book is a Persuasion Plan Workbook you can flip to as often as needed to see how to move through these steps, and then fill it out once you're ready.

But first I'm going to explain what pillars and proof points are and aren't.

THE THREE PILLARS

The three pillars are the three themes that are going to support your master narrative. You hear other brands' pillars all the time without realizing it. Why invest with Fidelity? Because of "performance, expertise, and variety." Google: "Our company, our commitments, our products." CVS: "Cost, quality, access." Those three words that follow a brand's tagline or master narrative are the pillars that their master narrative rests on. Every company has them, even if you don't know them because they live on the company's website and aren't used in their advertising. Ben & Jerry's are "Delicious ice cream, fair business practices, and environmental stewardship." Patagonia's are "Build the best product, cause no harm, and use business to inspire solutions to the environmental crisis."

Pillars are the three reasons why you will be able to deliver on your master narrative. Back to my example from chapter 2. I wanted to be known as the right person for this job, but if I couldn't prove that there were three reasons that made me the right one, reasons that mattered most to the people trying to hire me, the narrative "Lee is the right person for this job" would have fallen apart. In my case my pillars were "curious, scrappy, and eloquent," three qualities I could deliver on that would serve my employers. I'll help you find the three things that will support your master narrative.

PROOF POINTS

Frequently, people stumble over proof points and their role in persuasion because they confuse proof points, narrative, and story. To be persuasive, you need all three elements, but just one by itself can't do all three jobs. So often I hear people use proof points *in the place of* a master narrative or pillar, instead of *in support of.* Facts support your pillars; they can't replace them. For example, in the previous chapter I mentioned that there are 10,000 Muslims serving in the U.S. military today; that is not a story or a master narrative—it is simply a fact, a proof point. Remember how it didn't move the needle even a little bit?

Hundreds of times, clients have come to us and said, "If people knew these facts about us, we'd be just fine." As we discussed in the introduction, brands and people are often tempted to rely solely on facts when they want to persuade: "In the last century the earth has warmed .7 degrees Celsius." "The average woman will spend over $2,000 in a lifetime on sanitary products." "Ours was the first imported vodka." But without a story to carry them, facts rarely have that power. Especially now.

Once we have discovered your pillars, the goal will be to find the facts that will help you support them so that when you get into a productive (or heated) discussion, you'll have data to support your assertions. But facts alone won't create the essential emotional connection with your audience that will persuade them.

THE PHARMACEUTICAL INDUSTRY: A CASE STUDY IN EMPATHETIC PILLAR BUILDING

To find our way to the three pillars of your master narrative, we are going to make three key lists, from which everything you will need to persuade will flow. I am going to share with you this recent client example, so you can see this process in action all the way through, and then we're going to go back to the top and break it down in steps. So don't get too hung up on the *how* as you go through this case study. The how is coming.

Recently we were hired by a large pharmaceutical company—let's call it PharmaCare—because the industry as a whole is in crisis. In the debates about the Affordable Care Act, the pharmaceutical companies were painted as the villains, price gouging the consumers, the insurance companies, and the government. The narrative was that PharmaCare's greed endangered the lives of senior citizens and cancer patients. Of course, from the inside, this isn't how PharmaCare saw themselves at all. They were the solution people, on the forefront of trying to eradicate disease. So PharmaCare wanted help explaining to people, "Hey, we're not the bad guys here." But as we started working with them on this process, it became clear that they weren't seeing the consumers' problems, only their own.

They came to us believing—as many of our clients do—that if they just shared the facts with the world, everyone would understand. They were frustrated that prices were set by the insurance companies and they were getting blamed for it. They thought that if consumers understood that getting a drug to market takes years and costs millions and that the drug often fails to work, consumers would give them the benefit of the doubt. The problem was that they could say these things, of course, but this would not persuade their audience to think any differently about them. Because none of it is built on pillars that take the audience's needs, current beliefs, and obstacles to hearing their message into account.

They needed to understand all of the beliefs that consumers and patients had about pharma—all their baggage, everything that would get in the way of being heard. So we made a list of all the obstacles keeping their consumers from liking and believing them. Simply put, we needed to list all the bad stuff. The obstacles were:

1. People thought that pharmaceutical companies were greedy.
2. They thought that people who worked for pharmaceutical companies were manufacturing pills *and* pushing their brands to doctors and on television.

3. They didn't know that the companies were actually made up of scientists inventing drugs and trying to cure diseases. They thought hospitals and universities did that.

4. They were watching terrible news stories about price gouging with the EpiPen and Martin Shkreli's raising of the price of Daraprim by more than 5,000 percent while he was running the company then known as Turing Pharmaceuticals. These stories ended up being symbolic of the industry.

The next step was for us to practice active empathy to get into the head of their consumers. We needed to understand what they wanted from health care and pharma companies in general. So we made the second list. When it comes to health care and medicines, what is *important to the consumer*?

1. That the medicine is safe.
2. That it works.
3. That the patient has easy and consistent access to it.
4. That patients can afford it.
5. That new medicines are coming to address problems not yet solved.

Lastly, we needed to understand all the good things that this pharmaceutical company did. So we made the third list. Of the needs of the consumer, what could PharmaCare *deliver on*?

1. They offered special programs of discounts to those who couldn't afford their therapies otherwise.
2. They had the data to prove that their drugs work.

3. They had the data to prove they were safe.
4. They had a list of diseases they had helped to treat and more cures in the pipeline.
5. They had innovations that were helping with better dosages, better delivery mechanisms, and ways of reminding people to take their medicines so that they would be more effective.

Now we had three lists: the obstacles (or the bad stuff), the consumers' needs, and the things that PharmaCare could credibly do to remove those obstacles and meet those needs.

PHARMACARE'S LISTS

Customers' Obstacles	Customers' Needs	What PharmaCare Could Deliver
Greedy	Cures	Innovation
Expensive	Health	Treatments
Marked up	Affordability	Vaccines
Untrustworthy	Access	Better dosages
In bad company	Easier	

Once we had these three lists, it was time to find our pillars. The next step was to create a Pillar List. This is a list of every proof point about the strength and quality of the company we could think of to make our case.

1. PharmaCare has drugs for more than twenty-five different types of cancer in development.
2. Rewards programs, coupon programs, and rebate programs.

3. Assistance program for low-income families.
4. They had launched the most meaningful cancer drug in years.
5. They were focused on some of the toughest diseases out there: cancer, hepatitis C, cardiometabolic disease, antibiotic-resistant infection, and Alzheimer's disease.
6. They were on the front lines in the fight against emerging global pandemics.
7. They had invented vaccinations for life-threatening diseases.
8. They gave medicines away for free in developing nations.
9. They had two therapies in the pipeline for Alzheimer's.
10. They had new diabetes treatments for type 2 diabetes, allowing patients to take fewer medicines.
11. They had created nearly 75,000 jobs in the United States.
12. They had clinical trials going on life-threatening diseases such as advanced solid tumors, HIV, ovarian cancer, and prostate cancer.
13. They had well over $40 billion of annual revenue.
14. They spent more than $6.5 billion a year on R&D.
15. Sales increased by 10 percent that year.

Once we had this list, the next step was to go through it and cross off any items that reinforced the negative beliefs of our audience. For example, if the obstacle is that consumers think you're greedy, any proof points that tie back to monetary success or market share should be crossed out.

1. PharmaCare has drugs for more than twenty-five different types of cancer in development.
2. Rewards programs, coupon programs, and rebate programs.

3. Assistance program for low-income families.

4. They had launched the most meaningful cancer drug in years.

5. They were focused on some of the toughest diseases out there: cancer, hepatitis C, cardiometabolic disease, antibiotic-resistant infection, and Alzheimer's disease.

6. They were on the front lines in the fight against emerging global pandemics.

7. They had invented vaccinations for life-threatening diseases.

8. They gave medicines away for free in developing nations.

9. They had two therapies in the pipeline for Alzheimer's.

10. They had new diabetes treatments for type 2 diabetes, allowing patients to take fewer medicines.

11. ~~They had created nearly 75,000 jobs in the United States.~~

12. They had clinical trials going on life-threatening diseases such as advanced solid tumors, HIV, ovarian cancer, and prostate cancer.

13. ~~They had well over $40 billion of annual revenue.~~

14. ~~They spent more than $6.5 billion a year on R&D.~~

15. ~~Sales increased by 10 percent that year.~~

Then, in step 3, we highlighted all the proof points that mattered to the audience.

1. PharmaCare has drugs for more than twenty-five different types of cancer in development.

2. Rewards programs, coupon programs, and rebate programs.

3. Assistance program for low-income families.

4. They had launched the most meaningful cancer drug in years.

5. They were focused on some of the toughest diseases out there: cancer, hepatitis C, cardiometabolic disease, antibiotic-resistant infection, and Alzheimer's disease.

6. They were on the front lines in the fight against emerging global pandemics.

7. They had invented vaccinations for life-threatening diseases.

8. They gave medicines away for free in developing nations.

9. They had two therapies in pipeline for Alzheimer's.

10. They had new diabetes treatments for type 2 diabetes, allowing patients to take fewer medicines.

11. They had created nearly 75,000 jobs created in the United States.

12. They had clinical trials going on life-threatening diseases such as advanced solid tumors, HIV, ovarian cancer, and prostate cancer.

13. They had well over $40 billion of annual revenue.

14. They spent more than $6.5 billion a year on R&D.

15. Sales increased by 10 percent that year.

In step 4, we grouped the highlighted items into three categories. Those categories were our pillars.

For PharmaCare, the first pillar that emerged was *access*. A core need of their audience was being able to afford and get their medication when they needed it. In order to regain trust, that was something PharmaCare needed to stand for.

PHARMACARE MASTER NARRATIVE

Pillar One: Access	Pillar Two:	Pillar Three:
PP 1: Rebates and coupons	Proof Point 1:	Proof Point 1:
PP 2: Assistance to low-income families	Proof Point 2:	Proof Point 2:
PP 3: Global charity	Proof Point 3:	Proof Point 3:

The second pillar was *healing*. The company was investing millions of dollars in trying to find cures for their patients' ailments and illnesses. Every day they were trying to save their consumers' lives. That needed to be part of what they stood for in patients' minds.

PHARMACARE MASTER NARRATIVE

Pillar One: Access	Pillar Two: Healing	Pillar Three:
PP 1: Rebates and coupons	PP 1: Cancer drug	Proof Point 1:
PP 2: Assistance to low-income families	PP 2: Vaccines	Proof Point 2:
PP 3: Global charity	PP 3: Breakthroughs in diabetes treatment	Proof Point 3:

The third pillar was *innovation*. PharmaCare had clinical trials on drugs to treat or cure diseases like Alzheimer's, advanced solid tumors, HIV, ovarian cancer, prostate cancer, and hepatitis C.

PHARMACARE MASTER NARRATIVE

Pillar One: Access	Pillar Two: Healing	Pillar Three: Innovation
PP 1: Rebates and coupons	PP 1: Cancer drug	PP 1: Clinical trials on big diseases
PP 2: Assistance to low-income families	PP 2: Vaccines	PP 2: Clinical trials on chronic illnesses
PP 3: Global charity	PP 3: Breakthroughs in diabetes treatment	PP 3: Development of vaccines

Once we had these three pillars, each with its own set of proof points, we were able to ladder them up to their master narrative, which we will follow through with in the next chapter. But without these lists we would never have been able to find PharmaCare's three pillars because we wouldn't have been looking at the company from the consumer's perspective.

Now we'll slow down and go through each step in detail.

PERSUASION PREPARATION LIST 1. WHAT ARE YOUR AUDIENCE'S OBSTACLES TO PERSUASION?

You will be using the data you compile for these three lists for both your pillars *and* your master narrative. Getting clear on these three components of where you and your audience intersect is vital to crafting a successful message.

This first list of obstacles very much draws on the skills you built in parts one and two—it's an act of vulnerability and authenticity, but also one of empathy. You need to put yourself in your audience's place and look back at yourself clearly, which can be uncomfortable. But it will ultimately help you make your case to those who need persuading.

Their obstacles could also be that they've just never heard of you or love the product they're currently using; it doesn't necessarily need to be anything negative about you specifically. But list everything that might stand between you and your goal from their point of view. Here are some examples:

1. They think I'm overpriced.
2. They don't know what I stand for.
3. I'm not available near them.
4. I charge for shipping.
5. They disagree with my foreign policy.
6. They think I'm going to cost more than their current option.
7. They think switching to my product will be confusing and overwhelming.

In the Muslim American case we discussed in the previous chapter, it was imperative that we catalogued the haters' obstacles without judging them. This isn't always easy to do, especially when issues are as emotional as this. As simply as I can put it, we found through our interviews that their obstacles to persuasion were:

1. They had never met a Muslim person.
2. They had no idea what the actual tenets of Islam were.
3. They felt fearful.
4. They equated Islam with 9/11.

What are your audience's obstacles? If you want to be the PTA president, what will keep people from voting for you? Have not enough parents met you? Does your approach to fundraising make some people nervous because they don't understand it? Do they tend to prefer parents who don't also have full-time jobs? Have they never elected a man?

If you want people to encourage your state legislators to vote for gun control, what's keeping them from speaking out for gun control? Maybe the obstacle is that they were raised in a family of gun owners. That's tradition for them. Maybe they see gun control as a slippery slope. If you take that right from them, what else are you going to take away? Maybe the obstacle is that they don't want government telling them what to do.

What you must understand is that for this list to be helpful, it must be *their* problems with you, not *your* problems with them. Successful persuasion is about inhabiting the other person and looking at the issue solely from their perspective.

A few years ago, a foreign car company we'll call AutoCo hired us because their reputation for safety in the marketplace was suffering. After extensive focus groups, we went in to AutoCo and listed what all their consumers' problems with them were: "One, people no longer trust your vehicles are safe. Two, consumers don't think of you as actual people behind the brand. Three, they think having an AutoCo automobile means giving up some comforts and style. And four, they want to support American cars."

Oddly, of the four main problems we listed, the only one AutoCo was actively trying to solve was the fourth. They were trying at the time to be American. They had maps in every showroom of how many employees they had in America. They also talked about how the popular mid-size vehicle had more American parts than any other car. It was all true but didn't ring as authentic to their audience or solve their audience's problem with buying a foreign car. After listing all their genuine strengths, we said, "You're never going to be American, that's not your story." So we eliminated that as a contender for one of their three pillars.

Because they cared so deeply and wanted us to truly understand them and their organization, they invited us to tour the factories and meet the engineering teams. What was immediately apparent was that inside the organization, people were so confused. They knew they were really good at what they did. On the floor, employees kept saying to us, "But don't people know we're number one in QDR?" which stands for quality, dependability, and reliability. What we realized in that moment was that they didn't fully understand the problem that people had with their brand because they couldn't see it. They were in their own world making these cars.

Which is why this step of getting in touch with and listing all your audience's obstacles or problems is so important. Otherwise you're no better off than the class president running on "Vote for me: I'm awesome!"

PERSUASION PREPARATION LIST 2. WHAT'S IMPORTANT TO YOUR AUDIENCE?

This is a critical juncture where we frequently see clients go wrong. They get very focused on how they want to be seen, what they want to be known as, what position they want to occupy in the marketplace, instead of focusing on what their target audience *needs*. Politicians do this, too. "I'm the family candidate." "I'm the values candidate." The narrative is about them, not the voters. Hillary Clinton's campaign message "I'm with her" was heard by many voters as

"Vote for me because it's time a woman did this job," which translated to some as essentially "I want to make history." But she never explained how the voter would directly benefit. If a candidate never succinctly explains with a powerful master narrative what's in it for voters, he or she won't resonate.

Here's an example of shifting this thinking. Let's say I'm overwhelmed at work and what I want to do is ask my boss for another hire. I could go in and say, "I'm overworked. I need help." But that's all about me and my needs. He could respond, "Are you not doing your job properly?" It could get contentious. Instead I should slow down and ask myself, "What would benefit *him* and the organization? How can I frame my request in a way that will be heard as considering *his* needs?" *I'm knee-deep in paperwork, which takes me away from serving clients. If I'm not serving the clients, that could put the company in peril.* That is most likely his biggest concern, the health of the company. Now I'm looking at how I can meet *his* needs through what I want to persuade him of, rather than how he can meet mine. So I could say, "I really want to get somebody else in here because I think it's going to make the organization more efficient, productive, and profitable." I'm framing the argument based on what benefits my boss, so he's much more likely to say yes.

This is where empathy comes back in, because this isn't where *your* values matter, but where *their* values do. For climate change, our audience valued the environment, but they also valued freedom from government interference and autonomy. Tying this back to values-based empathy, we needed to address liberty/oppression, *not* care/harm. To be effective, our argument had to rest on pillars that would support those values.

AutoCo invited us to meet some of the engineers who designed their family car. One engineer told us how he drove around the country for *two years* before the redesign, watching how parents used the car, trying to understand the needs of the people they were designing for. They observed what parents did at pickup, at drop-off, at sports meets, at tailgates. The engineers saw, they watched, they witnessed, and one of the things they observed was that often kids' backpacks go at their feet, which kids and parents like because the kid can reach for whatever he needs without the parent needing to take their eyes off the road. But while everybody in test rides got in the back and said, "Wow, I have all this legroom," they didn't have a giant backpack on their feet.

So AutoCo decided they were going to be the first car manufacturer to make adjustable back seats. You could have the third row up or, if there was nobody in the third row, you could collapse it and adjust the placement to give kids more legroom.

Then as we were standing there, this woman who worked in communications for the engineering team jumped in and said, "Oh, you think that's interesting? I came to work the other day and put my sunglasses down and said, 'I'm so tired of my sunglasses holder not holding my sunglasses.'

"The engineers were stunned. They said to me, 'We tested that. When we designed the car, we bought every sunglass on the market!'"

So she took them down to her car and showed them that sunglasses styles had changed and the new ones didn't fit the old holders. Then she said, "By the way, I'm so sick of cars being designed for men. If you would just make a place for me to put my purse." Again, they were floored. So they designed the next version of the car to have a bigger sunglasses holder and room to put your purse under the seat.

Then another engineer said to us, "You know, we invented the first cup holder. Our engineers went to every country AutoCo cars were sold, bought every go-cup in every size, and tested all of them to make sure they fit."

As we made lists of what their customers valued, it became clear that AutoCo took the needs of its customers seriously. This would most likely be one of their master narrative pillars, the ones that would persuade consumers to trust AutoCo again.

PERSUASION PREPARATION LIST 3.
WHAT CAN YOU AUTHENTICALLY DELIVER ON?

We have all seen brands that simply try to tell us what they can deliver on but have given zero thought to what we as consumers need. Same for politicians, even on the local level. A friend of mine recently had a mayoral candidate running on rehabilitating her local waterfront into a dining and entertainment hub, but the town was having a pressing problem with opioids, so no one cared about the waterfront. Not only did the candidate lose, but she came off as woefully out of touch. Think of it like giving a gift the recipient doesn't want. We've all been there. Not only are you disappointed, but it also feels hurtful. You don't feel *seen*.

Our next responsibility is to look at the first two lists and ask ourselves, What can we realistically and consistently solve for our audience? Take the list of all your audience's problems with your goal and the list of what is important to them and *then* map it against what you're best at.

Don't try to do something for your audience that will make them feel like you haven't looked at the issue from their point of view. If what you can deliver on in this column doesn't match up with anything in the first two lists, it won't be persuasive.

In the case of AutoCo, they were actually best at safety, best at designing their cars with their users in mind, and best at hiring engineers who think about every last detail. They could deliver on all three of their consumers' needs. But they weren't telling that story. In this business, we always say if you aren't telling your story, someone else will. That's what AutoCo needed to bring to the forefront, because those qualities solved their consumers' problems and aligned with their values.

YOUR FIVE-STEP PILLAR PROCESS

Using the insights you've gained through making your three lists, you will be able to move quickly and efficiently through this part.

Step 1: List all the different ways you could argue your point to your audience. Imagine sitting across from the person you're persuading and listing all the reasons, all the things that you could say, that might convince them. It could be twenty, thirty, or even fifty points long—every argument for your case you can make. What are all the things that we can say about this drug? What are all the things we can say about this company? What are all the arguments we can make against regulation? List all the ways—no matter how small or seemingly tangential—you can think of to make your argument. You want a larger narrative to emerge, and tiny details might end up being part of a bigger whole, like AutoCo and the cup holders.

Step 2: Cross off any arguments or evidence that reinforce any of your audience's obstacles. In the case of the bank discussed in chapter 2 that was trying to recover from the financial crisis, we crossed out "Didn't own the subsidiary that made the bad loans at the time," because while this was true, it aroused suspicion. Why did they buy a bank with bad practices? How did they plan to profit from that? It didn't inspire trust.

Step 3: Circle all the proof points that align with what matters to your target. Now that you have your list of your audience's values and have given real thought to their views on you and your issue, you will readily know which ones will resonate with them.

Step 4: Group those proof points until you get to three discrete categories. See what patterns emerge. What you are looking for are the three lead categories. Each category will be a potential "frame" for your argument, the larger theme of your master narrative. Note that not all of the proof points will fit one of the three; some will get tossed out at this phase.

When we went through the process of framing AutoCo, we looked at our list of everything we could tell consumers about their quality, dependability, and reliability and identified three categories these facts and stories fell into. These were what we could talk about authentically that might persuade someone that AutoCo cars were still safe.

1. AutoCo engineers are teams of real people who drive these cars themselves and care deeply about the driver experience.

2. They have an incredible record of innovation and attention to detail.

3. The culture of AutoCo is one that gives back by sharing their knowledge.

Step 5: Polish the language in the three categories so the elements become memorable. AutoCo's pillars of customer-oriented design (everything they do to make their cars great today), innovation (everything they do to make their cars great for tomorrow), and community service (everything they do to cement ongoing relationships with their consumer and community) became Today, Tomorrow, and Together.

When we went through the third list, it became easy to cross out items like profitable and eco-friendly, because while those things were true, they didn't address the audience's core needs.

BUTTRESSING THE PILLARS WITH PROOF POINTS

For AutoCo's three pillars of safety, innovation, and community service, what were their proof points? For safety, it was that 90 percent of cars that have been built by AutoCo in the last twenty years are still on the road today. For the innovation pillar, we could point out that the engineers spent two years on average on the road before they set pen to paper designing a car. For community service, it was that they lend out their engineers to forty nonprofit and at-risk organizations a year to help them streamline and monetize their operations.

If you can't fill these columns with at least three supportive facts, you're probably going in the wrong direction and just saying something that's empty. Return to the three preparation lists to pick a new pillar.

CURATING AND STRESS TESTING

The reason we are trying to pare down the list to the three strongest proof points for each pillar, as opposed to ten or twenty, is that more information doesn't necessarily make a stronger case when it comes to persuasion. More proof points don't substantiate your pillar; they just overwhelm your audience.

Hillary Clinton had "137 Reasons to Vote for Hillary" on her website to support her experience pillar. But it was too much information for her supporters to be able to remember and disseminate on her behalf. When people are presented with more information than they can comfortably remember, they feel confused. Studies have shown that we avoid what confuses us. A lot of financial services companies are guilty of this right now. If you go to their website to figure out what they stand for and why you should invest with them, it becomes impossible. There are eighty-seven menu options and you can't find your way to what you want. In contrast, a handful of proof points make a pillar memorable, which is the goal. If your audience can remember your proof points and tell others about them, you will win.

Frequently we see this inability to whittle down the number of points when it comes to companies that support a wide array of charitable endeavors. Frequently they are all over the map and don't always ladder up to clearly supporting a pillar of community investment, which is one that would matter to their audience. For example, McDonald's wanted to offset the obstacle of the media story that their food isn't healthy for their customers, so on their website they touted the Ronald McDonald House, their healthy menus, and their investments in inner cities. But when the efforts are so dispersed, they become meaningless.

In persuasion, barraging your audience with too much information puts the onus on your audience to hold too much in their heads. People want to feel smart. They want to feel as if they've wrapped their brain around something as opposed to just barely scratching the surface of it.

So once you have your three pillars and nine curated proof points, it's time to start testing it. Run it by as many people as you think makes sense. Say: "I want to stand for these three things and here is why," and then concisely list your proof points. Then ask them if they think what you've said seems plausible, authentic, and memorable. Is it persuasive?

If not, take their feedback and go back to your lists and try a new pillar.

You may have to do a few rounds of this before you hit on the three that resonate with your audience. Once you do, you'll be ready to move on to chapter 6, evolving your pillars into your master narrative, and from there we'll learn how to tell the stories that communicate your narrative and weave in the proof points to support it. Then you'll be unstoppable.

6

YOUR MASTER NARRATIVE

Curly: Do you know what the secret of life is? [holds up one finger] This.

Mitch: Your finger?

Curly: One thing. Just one thing. You stick to that and everything else
don't mean sh*t.

Mitch: That's great, but what's the one thing?

Curly: [smiles] That's what *you've* got to figure out.   —*CITY SLICKERS*

Now that you have filled in your Persuasion Master Narrative sheet
with your three pillars and nine proof points, the master narrative
should evolve authentically from the things that are the most important to your target audience and that you can deliver on.

But how do you build that up to your One Thing? How do you
take these three pillars and turn them into meaningful change—
convincing your audience to become pro-life or pro-choice? How do
you take three pillars and turn them into climate change action?
That's what this chapter is about. How you find the one thing you
want to be known for. After doing the exercises in chapter 5, you
aren't going to make the mistake so many do because your master

narrative won't be built off what matters to you. It's now being built off what matters to your audience, and you have all the facts underneath it that are authentically true and resonant.

THE MASTER NARRATIVE IN EVERYDAY LIFE

Whether or not we're running for office, we all have a master narrative. You have one in your family, in your workplace, in your community; if you're not shaping it, others do. "Ask her to chair the fundraiser, she always gets it done." "Don't ask him to handle the ski rentals, he's unreliable." "Don't tell him anything, he's the neighborhood busybody." "Let's leave her off the committee, she'll make everything too complicated." "Don't invest in his taco truck, he's bad with money." "Be sure to include her, she thinks of everything."

Run your mind over everyone you know, and you probably have a one-sentence summation of them just like above. You certainly know when others have one about you. Think how frustrating it is when you feel like the master narrative people have about you is outdated or just plain wrong. Go back to the example of my 360-degree review in chapter 2. I thought my master narrative at work was *closer,* but that wasn't how I was perceived.

Your master narrative is that one thing about you or your brand that expediently embodies the critical emotional need you are going to fulfill for your audience. Everyone is telling a story. You want to have the shortest, most memorable one. When a new mom reenters the workforce, she needs a new master narrative, one that acknowledges her time away but positions it as a strength, one that allays any concerns about her priorities but doesn't misset expectations. Something like "I'm so excited to bring everything I've learned about consumer decision-making back into my career. Moms are the number one most targeted market, and it was invaluable to be on the other side for a few years."

When I moved out of the city, I wanted to create a new master narrative about myself as a neighbor. In the city, my master narrative had been "Lee Carter is a great neighbor because she keeps to herself." Now it needed to be "Lee Carter is a wonderful member of this community." So I started by inviting all our neighbors to a cocktail party when we moved in, with a note letting them know we were going to have a little work done and apologizing for any disruption, along with my number to call in case there was any noise. Then when I saw my neighbors, I let each person know one thing I would happy to do to help the community—garden, dog-walk, carpool. It was authentic to me. I was not going to bake pies, because I can't bake. But I could let people know that if they needed a cup of Marsala or they were running late on their way home from work and needed their dogs let out, I was their girl.

MASTER NARRATIVES FOR BRANDS

AutoCo had wanted to stand for quality, dependability, and reliability, but QDR isn't sexy. Their brand stories were awesome, but by themselves, each one might not be enough. We needed to find the master narrative that would support each one of the stories and show how scalable QDR was across everything that they did, the One Thing that made it all hang together in a way that is framed around the customer.

Once we had their three pillars, which we polished to "AutoCo, today, tomorrow, and together," we had to find their north star. And all our research told us that consumers, investors, and influencers were drawn to AutoCo because they've thought of everything their consumer needs—from the smallest things like cup holders and legroom to the biggest things like the future of mobility. Their cars, their culture, and the way that they give back are all built for how we live. So that is their new north star. "AutoCo: Built for how you live." Because people want to know that when they buy or invest in AutoCo, it will be quality. It will be intuitive. It will work. And it will last. All these facts and stories stacked up to a master narrative that satisfies that core emotional need of their consumers.

For the Muslim American organization, once we had our three pillars—purpose (their origin stories), people (their personal stories), and actions (things they were doing as the fabric of their communities)—we were able to stack them up to the master narrative "Reasons why I'm here." We were able to summarize it all and distill it down to something that mattered to them and was very different from what they would have ended up with if they hadn't gone through this exercise.

For PharmaCare, we knew from the pillars that there was a bigger quality of invention that consumers needed to associate with the brand. As we started to play with how to articulate that, we thought, *Well, we could say they've got the best R&D. Or we could say they're invested in your quality of life. Or we could talk about how they're innovative.* But what we hit on that got the best response was anything around invention. Then we started to play. "Finding cures to change the world." "See beyond impossible." "Live to cure." "Curing beyond impossible." With these we knew we were heading in the right direction. But we didn't distill it down to "Exploring for cures; adding years to your life and life to your years" until the next round.

Once PharmaCare adopted that new master narrative, "Exploring for cures; adding years to your life and life to your years," they went from the least innovative company in the eyes of consumers to rated number two most innovative in less than a year. That's a huge shift and an important one. It means they finally hit on a narrative that resonated with their audience, that hit the right note emotionally and shifted their message from one about the company to one that addressed the core need of the consumer—to feel cared for and cured.

MASTER NARRATIVES IN POLITICS

Where so many people go wrong is picking a master narrative that focuses on what they want to be known for but doesn't strike that emotional chord with their audience. We see this frequently in politics, where I do so much analysis for the cable news networks. Hillary Clinton's master narrative was "Hillary for America." And her lead pillar was experience. The problem there is that both are all about *her*, not all about us.

Knowing you've picked the candidate who has the most experience makes you feel a little good about yourself, but thinking you've picked the candidate who is going to change everyone's lives for the better makes you feel euphoric. When we tested "Make America Great Again," it consistently filled Trump's supporters with hope and made them feel like they had some control over their futures. Again, however you voted, it's important in the context of this conversation to understand that "Make America Great Again" is a master narrative that is almost impossible to beat. Obama had "Hope and Change We Can Believe In." That was equally powerful. Reagan had "Morning in America." But in 2016 none of the other candidates from either party had a master narrative that came close to "Make America Great Again" for effectiveness. I say that because it's important to hold up examples of the power of a master narrative to persuade and then transform those you've persuaded into your evangelists.

YOUR FIVE-STEP MASTER NARRATIVE PROCESS

Now it's time to discover your master narrative. By methodically moving through these five steps you will be able to uncover the language that will resonate with your audience and then start doing the work for you. Take the time at each step to sit with the language and the message as they're evolving to see how they feel. Above all, don't get frustrated. Sometimes it takes several rounds to find the perfect master narrative. But once you know what it is that makes a great master narrative, you won't settle for anything less than one that is persuasive.

STEP 1. WRITE A SENTENCE THAT SUMMARIZES YOUR PILLARS

This is where we put the pillars up on the wall and start thinking about all the things we could say that might encompass all three. If you're AutoCo and you want to persuade your audience you stand for QDR, or if you're Pepsi and you want to be known as a healthier company, if you're a Republican and want to be seen as altruistic, or a Democrat who wants to be seen as fiscally responsible, or if you're just trying to persuade your mother-in-law to let you host Thanksgiving, the process is the same.

For example, for PharmaCare it was "We are a cost-effective company that prioritizes finding cures and treatments to save our patients' lives." Once we had AutoCo's three pillars, we could say, "We are a car company that builds for today and tomorrow and shares that know-how with our communities." This led to us putting potential master narrative language on the board like "Our passion is your progress," and "It takes a village," and "Cars built for how you live," and "Engineered for humanity." "Built for how you live" ended up being the winning one because when we tested it there was just something bigger about it than the other ones. But it doesn't need to be fine-tuned at this point. The goal here is simply getting the three pillars to start working together in one sentence.

Not every master narrative needs to be a pithy tagline. If you are trying to persuade your neighbors to tie up their newspapers and cardboard with string for recycling so your building stops getting fined, putting up signs in the elevator and basement showing tied cardboard with the words *77 Lafayette, We Do It the Right Way Every Time*, might be enough to inspire them to feel a sense of pride in taking care of their garbage properly and persuade them to be better stewards of their building. But if you're running for local office or need to make a sustained push in your workplace for new policies, having language that you and your supporters can effortlessly repeat will mean thinking of all the ways you can verbalize your categories until you find one that sings.

STEP 2. THINK ABOUT WHY IT MATTERS

Now, how do you find your One Thing? You take this sentence and go back to what matters most to the person or people you're trying to persuade—and think about what's in it for them. I had a client who used to say her consumers' favorite radio station was WIIFM: *What's in it for me?* Ask yourself, Which benefits of what you're offering are the most important to them? For example, let's say you want to sell an across-the-board tax cut and you have gotten your three pillars down to "A tax cut that will simplify the tax code, stimulate the economy, and put money in American pockets." The question is then, Why does that matter to your audience? I find that if you ask yourself, "So what?" or "Why does that matter?" about five times, you will get to your answer. Here's what that would look like:

a. A tax cut will simplify the tax code, stimulate the economy, and put money in American pockets.

Why does that matter?

b. Because if people have more money, they'll spend more.

Why does that matter?

c. Because when people spend more money, companies make more money and can hire more people.

Why does that matter?

d. Because then there will be more jobs for more people, benefiting the American worker.

Now you have your message. "I am proposing tax relief for job creation and economic growth—or jobs and growth tax reform." When I tested these options with voters, the messaging that resonated was the one that immediately spoke to why it *mattered to them*.

When a food company famous for an American pantry staple wanted to update their language and messaging, we wanted to uncover what was at the root of their proof points. There was a lot you could say about this brand with which we'd all grown up. You could focus on the fact that their product was both nutritious and easily available, that it was comforting when you're sick, that it's a staple in homes across America. You could lean into heritage, playing up the fact that it's been around for 150 years. But to get to the essence of what the brand is really about, we needed to go deeper and figure out what these facts have in common. What emotions do they actually generate? How do they make people feel? The pillar sentence we were working with was "Cozy Company is a 150-year-old brand delivering nutritious food with ease."

a. Cozy Company is an iconic American brand that's been around for 150 years.

Why does that matter?

b. Because if it's been around that long, it must be dependable.

Why does that matter?

c. Because I want to trust what I feed my family.

Why does that matter?

d. Because in turn my family trusts me to make decisions about what goes in their bodies.

Why does that matter?

e. Because that's how I show them my love and care.

Now we had their new master narrative: "Crafted with Care." The length of time they've been around, a cold fact, gets infused with emotion when it becomes about trust and family.

As you go through this exercise, what you are offering your audience can go from an impersonal statement to an emotional one. It can go from something that doesn't matter to something that matters deeply to them—and then you will find your One Thing, and within it, your master narrative.

For AutoCo we had the framing of problem-solvers. So we asked, Why does it matter? Well, because then there are no problems, only improvements. Why does that matter? Because if I see all the problems, I can imagine the solutions. Why does that matter? It means that consumers are always going to get what they need. Why does that matter? Because it's going to be built for how they live.

STEP 3. CHECK THE SENTENCE AGAINST
YOUR THREE LISTS AND CORE EMOTIONS

Now you've listed all your points, categorized them, and asked, "Why does it matter?" over and over to distill your categories down to something that will be important, that will resonate with whomever you are trying to persuade. The next step is to look at your three Persuasion Preparation Lists and make sure this new sentence doesn't reinforce any obstacles, that it matters to your target audience, and that you can deliver on it.

Customers' Obstacles	Does your master narrative reinforce any of them?
Customers' Needs	Does your master narrative address their needs?
What You Can Deliver	Does your master narrative fit with the things you can deliver?

The next step is asking, "What core emotion am I tapping into?" Many of the potential master narratives we had for AutoCo sounded good, but they didn't tap into the core emotion we needed to elicit, which was "I feel safe."

So now we match the list of potential master narratives up against the feeling that you want people to have. You don't need to test them right away. You can pretend to be your target audience and *imagine* how they will feel when they hear each contender. We wanted the people who were nervous about Muslim Americans to feel heard and at ease. We wanted the climate change deniers to feel respected and inspired.

The key here is figuring out which emotion it will bring up without judging that emotion. This is where empathy comes back in.

STEP 4. TEST IT AGAINST THE FOUR *PS*

In his book *The Language of Trust*, my partner Michael Maslansky writes about the four *Ps*, which are the criteria that every successful message must be measured against. Take your new master narrative and ask yourself:

1. Is it *plausible*?

   Is it specific, and can you deliver on it? Can your audience *believe* you can deliver on it? Plausible language is the key to being believed. In order for language to be plausible, it must meet a few criteria. First, it needs to be neutral—meaning it can't be a judgment statement. Second, plausible language is complete. It represents the good and the bad of who you are much like we talked about earlier in chapter 2. And finally, plausible language avoids absolutes, superlatives, and overly bold claims.

   For example, we worked for a food and beverage company that is in the cross hairs of the obesity debate. The CEO wanted to go out and say, "You are all wrong. We are committed to a healthy future. A healthy America. And healthy children." I probably don't need to tell you the reaction of consumers, but let's just say when we tested this statement, there were audible sighs and noticeable eye rolls in the room. But when we changed the word from *healthy* to *healthier*, we got a completely different response. One is plausible. One is not. One gave them credit. One got them dismissed.

   It isn't that the statement can't be audacious—companies do and should set audacious goals all the time—but it needs to feel plausible to your audience or you'll lose them at the outset.

2. Is it *positive*?

Imagine you were a credit card company and you needed to write a script for your call center representatives to collect money from a delinquent customer. A negative frame would be "If you don't make these six consecutive minimum payments, we may keep the penalty annual percentage rate on your account indefinitely." If you were to frame it in positive terms, you would say something like "If you make on-time payments for the next six billing cycles, this penalty will go away. You will return to your original APR."

The same applies if you are entering a debate. I often say that the person who is reacting isn't acting and that means they are losing. Think about the framing we talked about for climate change. We found that by taking a fear-based or negative approach like "We can't afford to let this happen. We are only years away from catastrophe," we alienated most of the audience we were trying to persuade. But when we framed it around the positive reasons to pay attention, we got people on board.

3. Is it *personal*?

There is only one thing that matters—the audience. But when we are attempting to persuade someone, our instinct is often to talk about ourselves. Think about financial advisers who say things like "I have my CFP and Series 7 and

12," or "I have over a billion in assets under management," or "I have more than twenty years of experience." While all these things may be true—and all these things may be interesting—they aren't necessarily important to the target audience. If that same financial adviser said, "I would love to have a conversation to understand your long- and short-term goals. I want to spend some time listening to you so that I can create a custom plan to help you reach them," you'd be much more open to being persuaded to give him your business. A master narrative like "We're number one" will be effectively persuasive only if you're making your audience feel smart for picking the best company. Is your narrative empathetic? Is it serving them?

4. Is it *plainspoken*?

Is it in the language of your target audience? No jargon? Ask yourself, *How can I make it pithier? How can I make it smarter? How can I make it stronger?* Play with it so that it's memorable. Whether it's coming out in headline form or employing alliteration or rhyming, this is your anchor statement. It doesn't have to be totally polished, it just has to be memorable, and comfortable for you to say over and over again. So wherever the conversation goes, it can come back to what you're trying to convey. This point sounds obvious, but we see jargon everywhere we go. The more familiar you are with an issue, product, or company, the more jargon you have picked up. So make sure to check for this.

For example, we recently helped an insurance company with their language and made a few tweaks to be sure that it was plainspoken:

You say	They hear	Instead say
Network	What network are we talking about? What's in my network?	Preferred doctors and hospitals
Premium	Like it's special or extra costly?	Monthly payment
Clinical guidelines	For what clinic?	Treatment guide-lines

STEP 5. TAKE IT TO YOUR ADVISORY
BOARD AND TEST IT FOR RESONANCE

So now you should have a good master narrative. If you can't pick up the phone and hire us, you still should do research to be sure you are being heard in the way you want to be heard. Email some options to friends and colleagues. Or post them on Facebook and ask for votes. Run it by your friends in the dog park. Send out a SurveyMonkey or Google Forms.

In running these by people, you might find that you have the right theme but not the right phrasing. Some words are triggers. We initially thought focusing on AutoCo's problem-solving would be a great thing, but then the audience focused on the fact that we were raising the specter of problems.

Occasionally when we go through this process, a couple of different triggers pop up that we get worried about. One is what we call a *contradiction alert*, which means something you might want to say, but you can't authentically say and could get in trouble for.

Like the bank that wanted to be seen as consumer driven while they were on a foreclosing spree. Your point might sound good and it might be what the person wants to hear, but you have to go back to what customers think about you. I put a star next to anything that might cause people to say, "I don't buy that coming from you."

Then we go through and ask, Are there any language land mines? In the AutoCo example, the word *problem* would be a potential land mine, because the idea of bringing up a problem is risky. Sometimes you have to bring up the problem to get to the answer, and that's okay. But as you're going through the list, it's important to consider those two potential traps and understand the risks involved if you're a business. How you can still be authentic and say the same thing? For the bank it was saying, "We're spending time listening to our customers, and that's why we're changing *x, y, z*." This was a different way of articulating that they're customer driven and it took away that contradiction alert.

When you star those potential contradictions and land mines, you might then want to spend some more time asking, "How else could I say this?" Or "Is there a way that I could say this in which it helps my authenticity?" Or you might realize, "That's a place I never want to go."

Which doesn't mean you *have* to make the safe choice every time. You just want to know exactly which choice you're making so you're not blindsided by your audience's reaction. For example, when women first heard the word *iPad*, most said, "That's a terrible name for a product."

We worked on a rewards credit card for a bank, and when we were going through this process, we listed all the benefits of the card, but what we never did was talk about the removal of obstacles. When we were going through this list, nothing sounded different from the hundreds of other rewards cards out there.

Then we read the fine print of all the cards, and we realized, "Maybe there's something in the 'no restrictions.' Instead of what it is, what is it removing?" That's when we got to "no hoops." But people had mixed feelings about this. If you took a bunch of your friends out to dinner and asked them their gut feeling about "no hoops," they might say, "A 'no hoops' rewards card? I don't know, do I want my card to be hoopy? I don't know. That language sounds different. I'm not sure . . . I want serious."

But at the same time, it stuck with people. There was something emotional about "no hoops" versus "cash back." "Cash back" was emotional the first time consumers heard it, but then it became ubiquitous, so we stuck with "no hoops" and the response was tremendous. So sometimes using slightly risky language isn't always a bad thing.

EVOLVING YOUR NARRATIVE

A great example of the successful evolution around a lasting master narrative is Barbie. We all grew up with Barbie; it was a beloved brand. But in recent years Mattel struggled as perception shifted to how Barbie objectifies women and how the doll creates an impossibly perfect model for girls to emulate. Yet many of us have such fond memories of growing up with Barbie.

What Mattel did a few years ago is get back to that One Thing: it was never about the doll, it was about the girl. They launched a campaign that reminded moms that the girls use the dolls to act out their dreams of adult womanhood, all their ambitions and hopes. The campaign showed little girls imagining themselves as professors, veterinarians, soccer coaches, and executives; it brought you right back to that moment where you were a girl with a dream. That's a master narrative that people can rally behind. And it worked. They persuaded moms that the purchase of a Barbie doll was an investment in their daughters' futures.

MASTER NARRATIVES HAVE THE
POWER TO EFFECT CHANGE

Persuasion lasts longer than marketing or advertising because we're changing people's minds. In 2015 the brand Always launched a campaign called #LikeAGirl that asked the very powerful question "At what age does doing something 'like a girl' become an insult?" In 2014 Pantene started a campaign called #ShineStrong that focused on getting women to stop apologizing all the time. The Pantene commercial actually raised awareness about our female culture of saying, "Sorry," all the time and it changed behaviors in women. I'm not sure if it sold more of their hair products, but there was something really persuasive about seeing ourselves in action. It brought an awareness and a change. Like the 2019 Nike "Dream Crazier" campaign, these ads tapped into a powerful emotion, and then the consumer was doing the work for the brand by forwarding the ads and ensuring they went viral. Now instead of just putting out another feminine hygiene commercial, you've actually done something for women.

In India, women do 90 percent of the chores around the house and men do 10 percent, but men almost never do laundry. So in 2015, Ariel, an Indian detergent brand owned by P&G, developed a campaign with BBDO called #sharetheload. Part of the campaign was a commercial where a father in India is reading a letter to his daughter, who is seen bustling about the house, multitasking on the phone as she takes care of her family. He says, "My little baby girl, you're all grown up now. You used to play house and now you manage your own house and your office. I am so proud, and I am so sorry. I never told you that it's not your job alone, but your husband's, too, but how could I have said it when I never helped your mom either." The father continues: "Your husband must have learned the same from his dad. . . . Sorry on behalf of his dad . . . sorry on behalf of every dad who set the wrong example." The video went viral. It was all people could talk about. In the following year more than 2.1 million men pledged to share the load and do the laundry—and Ariel's sales increased by more than 111 percent.

BRINGING IT ALL TOGETHER:
THE PILLARS AND THE MASTER NARRATIVE

Before we move on to part four, I want to show you what this looks like all together. For that, I will use a case study from one of the most exciting industries we work in: insurance. I jest. My point in using insurance as an example is to show you that this will work regardless of the topic or goal.

When we started our work together, Protection Corp believed that their target market didn't know that they existed, and their job as communicators was to introduce themselves as an insurance company who caters solely to the needs of the affluent. The funny thing was, that wasn't the problem at all. What we found was that while their target market was demographically affluent, according to their psychographics, they didn't see themselves that way.

So every time we talked about how Protection Corp was the original insurer of the affluent, all their target consumer heard was "Oh, so you're for this other rich guy that I know, not me. And you're so expensive because you need to be able to cover the superduper wealthy, which is not me." You could talk to the guy who owned a boat, but he knew a guy who owned two boats. Make sure there isn't a schism between how you see your target audience and how they see themselves—even if it's flattering!

Protection Corp felt that if they could just show the consumers how they needed more and better coverage, consumers would act. The problem was that nobody saw a pain point with the coverage they currently had but they would pay for a better experience. We helped Protection Corp understand the importance of showing how working with them would make their clients *feel*. It was less about offering better liability protection or more coverage for high-end items. Instead, when Protection Corp focused on the "ways to say yes to their customers"; when they talked about treating clients as people, not numbers on spreadsheets; when they talked about responding to claims within twenty-four hours and issuing checks in forty-eight hours—all of these statements spoke to a perceived pain point of what it's like should anything actually happen. Then their prospects wanted to learn more.

Here's the list of what mattered to their prospects:

- Service.
- Claims would be processed quickly.
- A company that won't sweat the details and nitpick over every line item.
- A company that won't require you to dig up receipts.
- A company that isn't going to approach the situation as if you have to have a battle and a negotiation.
- A firm that is actually doing what's right.

When they listed what they could do:

- Service.
- Claims would be processed quickly.
- They wouldn't sweat the details and nitpick over every line item.
- They wouldn't require you to dig up receipts.

- They weren't going to approach the situation like a battle and a negotiation.
- An exclusive high-end offering.
- A variety of coverage.
- Expertise.

Their proof points were:

- Insuring affluent people for over a hundred years.
- All of the coverage limits are the highest in the industry.
- Their claims adjusters are able to approve your claim.
- If they were vague in their contract, they'll give you the benefit of the doubt, and they'll pay it.
- Able to pay claims in forty-eight hours.

After going through those lists, we came up with three pillars. Pillar 1 was "We look for ways to say yes." Pillar 2 was "We look for ways to do more," and Pillar 3 was about "inclusive coverage."

Then we arrived at their master narrative: "With Protection Corp you can raise your expectations."

Lastly, we found the stories to support it. One great example was a complimentary service they offered for wildfires. If a wildfire is heading toward a client's zip code, they will send a team to their home to clear away brush and even cover the family's home in a fire-retardant gel. They told a story of one family whose home was spared. The fire came through the town, but their home didn't go up in flames. When the family returned, Protection Corp had already come back and cleaned off the gel, so all they had to do was open their door and go back to life as usual.

Ultimately, I leave you with this. Imagine you have thirty seconds in an elevator, or two minutes on a job interview, to make the impression that will get you what you want. Your master narrative is the one thing you can do for whoever you're trying to persuade, the one thing that they will remember and is meaningful to them. Master stories are dead-simple one-sentence embodiments of who you are that turn your audience into your brand ambassadors. If you're confident that you have built a story around your target audience, and you know them in your heart of hearts, then you just stick with it. You adapt around your master narrative, but you don't change your One Thing.

PART 4

STORY

7

MAKE IT VISUAL

I believe in a visual language that should be as strong as the WRITTEN word.
                                                        —DAVID LaCHAPELLE

Before we move into how to tell a story that sells, let's take stock of your persuasion process thus far. You have a big vision you are excited to persuade people of and you know the person you need to persuade intimately and empathetically. You have crafted three pillars for your argument and a master narrative that makes your audience feel that your vision is their solution. You're backing up that master narrative with no more than three succinct proof points per pillar. Now you're ready to master the last two components of great persuasion technique that will help you close the deal: visual language and story.

In my old office, I had a wall of Post-it notes with my least-favorite words. The top two offenders were *moist* and *dangle,* words that make me, and most people, cringe. When I see an ad with those words in it, I honestly question if the company wants to sell their product. When my last head shot was taken, those two Post-its ended up in the frame. Prospective clients would always ask me, "Why is your head framed by the words *moist* and *dangle*?!" and I would tell them about my office wall.

As our relationship progressed, I'd meet people higher in the chain of command, and they'd invariably say, "Lee! You're the woman with the wall of words!" It was such a memorable image they had shared it internally. It was becoming part of my master narrative. The wall was the symbol in the story of my decades-long commitment to curating language based on its visceral quality. And it told that better than my saying "I'm committed to curating language" ever could.

When my partner Keith Yazmir started here at the firm in 2006 at a senior level, he sensed from his first day that people were trying to make sense of what this new guy was all about. Instead of sitting everyone down and saying, "Hey, guys, relax—I'm not going to step on any toes, I'm here to have fun," which would have had the exact opposite effect, he sent out an email inviting the entire company to Thirsty Thursday in his tiny office. When we congregated in the seven-by-ten space, there was food, cocktails, and music, even decorations. It was a concrete, visual demonstration of his humor and personality. Not only did it break the tension, it shaped his entire tenure here. We all look forward to Keith's office parties and wry sense of humor.

Almost every day, I have to impress upon a client that telling their customers that they believe in something or are committed to something is almost useless without a clear visual to back it up. Because it's visuals that stick in our minds. We think in pictures. If you can plant a positive picture in the mind of whomever you're trying to persuade, you are that much closer to getting what you want.

We call these pictures symbols. A symbol can be a person, an object, or an action, but it needs to be concrete and tangible. It can't be conceptual. For example, immigration policy is conceptual, while walls are something everyone can picture. I understand that it pains half of you reading this book to hear it, but can you name any visual symbols associated with Hillary's 2016 campaign that the campaign chose? The visual symbol of the campaign was email. By not replacing that symbol in the voters' minds, she lost a key component of her persuasion strategy. Symbols have the visceral power to disrupt the conversation in a way that a longer story can't.

VISUAL LANGUAGE IN ACTION

The job of visual language is to plant one of your pillars in your audience's mind in a way that will stick. Which statement creates a clearer picture: "I'm a great editor" or "I have a rule: write once, edit three times"? "I'm a great project manager" or "I can't leave for the night until every box has a check mark next to it"?

When we were working on a beverage company's water-conservation initiative, we told them that instead of saying that you're saving millions of gallons, which starts to feel abstract, say that you're saving fifteen Olympic-sized swimming pools' worth of water. That gave their audience a visual symbol to go along with their claim, which made it far more memorable and allowed their consumers to repeat it, which is how the message penetrates.

Bounty has been "the quicker picker upper" for three decades. This is a master story that lasts because the corporation uses the same visual to back up the words: the wet paper towel catching the spill before it goes over the edge of the counter, and then still being strong enough to hold a bunch of grapes. The ads don't just tell us Bounty paper towels are strong; they show us that wet towel.

Visual language that sticks is more vital than ever because institutions have become meaningless. It used to be that a brand could get a high rating from J. D. Power and Associates or the *Good House-keeping* Seal of Approval and they'd put that information or symbol on their package and be made. Now you need good reviews on Amazon or Yelp or TripAdvisor, and the success of your business is in the hands of *all* your customers, not just a panel of objective experts. Studies have shown that consumers put more weight behind crowd-sourced reviews than professional reviews. That's not logical; that's emotional. So brands need to replace that visual endorsement with a powerful symbol that sticks in consumers' minds and resonates emotionally.

After the financial crisis, banks were perceived as having used opaque language to trick customers into signing adjustable rate mortgages without explaining that the payments would escalate eventually. People hadn't known that they were getting themselves in over their heads, didn't understand the terms of these adjustable rate mortgages, and felt they had been tricked. So one of our banking clients wanted one of their new pillars to be transparency, but the challenge was that transparency is an abstract concept. It's ambiguous, and it didn't necessarily address the problem of eroded trust. So, we asked ourselves, what would be a symbol of a commitment to transparency?

We played around with a lot of different options. We said, "We are no longer going to have footnotes. Footnotes are going to be in the same size font as everything else in our documents." Eventually we landed on the idea of a one-page summary document that would accompany every mortgage package moving forward, because we all know that when you buy a house, you have no idea what you're signing. "Here's one page that says in plain English at a fourth-grade level exactly what you're agreeing to."

Then we named it the Clarity Commitment. The Clarity Commitment stated that no matter what product or service you got from that bank, and no matter how complicated it was, whether it was a financial services instrument or a mortgage, you were going to get one page in plain English that summarized everything you were agreeing to.

Once that symbol was added, the initiative had a much bigger impact. That critical reputational driver substantially increased customer satisfaction. In other words, their customers now trusted them more to do the right thing, which was a big shift after the financial crisis.

When Starbucks brought CEO Howard Schultz back after years of declining market share, they didn't just say, "We're getting back to our roots" or "We're recommitting to quality." They closed all their stores nationwide for three hours to retrain every barista on making the perfect cup of coffee. It was a national news story, and those closed stores stuck in people's minds as a visual reminder of how much Starbucks cared. The results were worth waiting for.

When you're next making a claim, any claim, think about the most vivid image that conveys what you're trying to get across. Comb your mission and objective statements for theoreticals and transform them into tangibles.

THE JOB OF SYMBOLS

When symbols are used to support your master narrative, they can do one of two jobs. You will need your symbol either to *differentiate* you from a crowded marketplace or to *rehabilitate*. Either way, it needs to be memorable and emotionally resonant. I'll break down both categories and then teach you how to find yours on the following pages.

SYMBOLS THAT DIFFERENTIATE

Charities are especially adept at these, because for every cause, there are multiple ways to support it and a finite number of donors. Think about St. Jude Children's Research Hospital. They aren't primarily a treatment hospital—they're actually a research hospital. They have only twenty-seven beds, but they have made their pediatric patients their symbol because research is abstract. It's been incredibly effective— when you think of pediatric cancer, you think of St. Jude's.

When Purple launched their mattresses in 2016 into a crowded market of mattresses sold online, they invented something they called the egg test, where they barraged the internet with videos of sheets of glass being dropped onto their mattresses without smashing raw eggs resting atop them. Now what does this actually prove? Who knows? But it stuck in consumers' minds and boosted Purple to the top of the division. Tempur-Pedic has a full wineglass standing upright on one side of the mattress while someone jumps on the other side. That symbol was much more powerful than saying, "Our mattresses don't conduct motion." It was a symbol that solved their consumers' core need: a bed that would allow a sound sleeper to survive someone who tosses and turns.

The Gerber Baby is another wonderful example. It's a beautiful baby of ambiguous gender, a visual promise that if you choose their products, your child will also be a healthy, dimpled, smiling tot.

The Ivory Girl, Bioré nose strips, Gwyneth Paltrow's makeup-free selfies—beauty companies have historically understood the power of symbols to convert their audience. "Who wears short shorts?" Short shorts are a bright, fun image that lodges in your head without having to think about what hair remover actually smells or feels like.

The Wheaties athlete; the Keebler Elves; Snap, Crackle, and Pop—

these were all symbols that loomed large in their consumers' consciousness in the seventies and eighties. They personalized the second generation of factory-made food and overcame mothers' obstacles to buying packages for their home.

Today comparable symbols would be Kylie Jenner's lips.

SYMBOLS THAT REHABILITATE

Very often when a brand or a community or people are in crisis, it's because there is a negative symbol attached to them. To correct this, first you must go back to your list of audience obstacles to persuasion and ask yourself, *What are the current symbols my audience is associating with me?* This can be uncomfortable, even frustrating. But it's vital to make an honest assessment so you know where you're starting from. For AutoCo, the symbol that needed to be replaced was the faulty brakes. For the Muslim Americans, it was the lingering images of 9/11. For PharmaCare, it was pills. The problem with a pill is that it's small, it dissolves, and it's impossible to convince anyone that it's expensive to manufacture. It was a visual representation of all their consumers' obstacles. If we go back to my 360-degree review, the symbol that had been in my colleagues' head was my empty chair in the mornings. That was the symbol I had to replace in their minds. Or think of the Detroit auto manufacturers who had their CEOs take private planes to the congressional hearings on the 2008 bailout. There was very little they could say after that to erase that image.

Are you trying to run for local office as a fiscal conservative? Did you have a bouncy castle and fireworks at your last kid's birthday that could be seen for blocks away? That's the symbol you have to replace. Did your product sicken some people, malfunction, or backfire? Did you come back into the holiday office party with your skirt tucked into your Spanx? Make a list of every symbol, no matter how unfair or embarrassing, so you can find the perfect symbol to address and dispel it.

For AutoCo, as we looked back through our list of proof points of their commitment to excellence, innovation, and customer care, what stood out to all of us was the cup holder. It's a clear symbol of their master narrative, "Built for how you live." For the Muslim American organization, we talked about baseball, a quintessentially American symbol. Once you are picturing someone playing baseball, you are finding commonality with that person better than if the person said, "I'm American, just like you." With PharmaCare, the most powerful symbol of their master narrative was scientists in a lab working to find cures.

There are even symbols themselves that have negative connotations. Companies used to go on television handing out those oversize checks like the Publishers Clearing House sweepstakes. But there is so much skepticism now that when people see that on the news, it seems fake to them. They don't want to see the symbolic check, the potentially empty *promise* of help; they want to see the results. They say, "Show me the person back in their foreclosed home." "Show me the factory reopened." "Show me the person graduating from school." Ask yourself, How do I turn that symbol on its head, turn it into a real plus? How do I turn it into one of my pillars, into something that's going to be visual and flip that perception around?

ACTIONS AS SYMBOLS

Sometimes actions can serve as symbols. Listening is an excellent example. Consider when a candidate doesn't just *say* they are listening to voters, they hold a listening *tour*. Then instead of calling them town hall meetings or opportunities to meet the candidate, they call them listening sessions. Another example of an action symbol is a guarantee. Saying you stand by your product and offer refunds is one thing. Offering a guarantee is something different. Consider Walmart's Price Matching Policy. They don't just say, "We have the best prices anywhere." They don't just offer up their prices versus the competitor's; they will match the prices of others, which conveys, "We're so committed to being the most convenient, cost-effective place for you to shop that if you bring in a coupon from somewhere else, we'll match it." That's a symbol of their promise. Similarly, when Zappos first launched, it had to overcome the obstacle that people really need to try on shoes and most won't fit. So they made their "free shipping both ways" guarantee the bedrock of their persuasion—and it worked.

SYMBOLS THAT FAILED TO RESONATE

In 2015 Jay-Z bought and relaunched the music streaming service TIDAL. The idea of the service was to pay musicians higher royalties than any other service, returning a living income to the thousands of smaller musicians who have lost revenue due to Spotify, Pandora, and Apple. Celebrities like Madonna, Beyoncé, and Rihanna would throw their weight behind it, forcing the labels to support negotiating these better rates for other lesser-known artists. It was supposed to be an altruistic mission. The symbol should have been a musician in Nashville uploading their first song and making enough off of it to quit their shift waitressing. Instead, the campaign hinged on the symbol of the sixteen celebrity partners having a "secret" meeting at Jay-Z's Hamptons compound. It wasn't relatable or resonant, and to this day TIDAL has only a fraction of the users of the other streaming services.

CEO Ron Johnson had successful runs at both Apple and Target before joining JCPenney in 2011. The company had once been known for housewares and children's clothing—but amid the economic troubles and management changes it had lost its way. One of the first things the new CEO did was to develop a new strategy to rebrand themselves using the symbol of consistent pricing, essentially saying, "We're going to be consistently cheap." However, the problem that customers had with JCPenney, the reason consumers were choosing their competitors over them, was not just cost. In fact, many customers used to like to come to JCPenney for their sales. Taking away sales took away some of the incentive to visit the store. One of the bigger problems they had was that they didn't think JCPenney had the chic clothes they were looking for. However, at the same time that JCPenney launched their consistent pricing, they had also redesigned their stores and added new high-end designers like Joe's. But they didn't lead with that. It was at a time when Target was waffling a little and JCPenney could have created a symbol around being a better shopping experience. As Harvard Business School marketing expert Rajiv Lal put it in an interview with Harvard Business School Working Knowledge: "No matter what, someone has to articulate a new and improved strategy, but right now, amid all the distractions, that isn't happening. That is very bad news for a once significant retailer and the thousands of men and women who work there."* There were a number of different approaches JCPenney could have tried if they had tested their symbols against the list of what mattered most to their customers.

---

* Jim Aisner, "What Went Wrong at J. C. Penney?," Harvard Business School Working Knowledge, August 21, 2013, https://hbswk.hbs.edu/item/what-went-wrong-at-j-c-penney.

HOW TO FIND YOUR SYMBOL

Similar to the "Why does it matter?" exercise, when you have a persuading statement like "I'm tough on crime" or "Loyalty is our middle name," imagine someone asking you, "But how?" That will lead you to start thinking of *how* you are going to clearly demonstrate your value.

"We at Hilton care about your comfort."

But how?

"We're going to let you pick your pillow at check-in."

That pillow calls attention to your comfort better than Hilton's saying, "We care about your comfort."

Ideally you will want to find an image, a symbolic gesture, or visual language to underscore each of your pillars and your master narrative. To do that, take a look at your master narrative and your three pillars and answer the following questions for each:

1. What images or visuals best illustrate the theme or point you are trying to make? Here is some inspiration:

   a. *If you are trying to change someone's opinion of you, your brand, or your company:*

   What picture do you want your target audience to see in their mind's eye? If you are trying to change their minds, they probably have a very negative picture in their head. So if you are a restaurant that just had a food safety scare, what image do your customers have in their head? Is it people in the hospital after getting food poisoning? Is it rotten ingredients? Is it mice in the kitchen? You need to know exactly what the image is so that you can create an image that will counterbalance it. In this example, what would safety look like? Is it a clean kitchen? Is it fresh ingredients? Is it a family eating together? Is it a mother feeding her child the food? Is it parents choosing to have their child's birthday party at the restaurant? Be specific. And be able to paint that picture with words.

b. *If you are trying to create an image where there is none:*

You are launching a product in a totally new category. You are a start-up. Even more challenging still, you are launching a totally new product unlike anything people have used before. What is your symbol? There are a few things that you can draw on here. First, what problem are you trying to solve? Think about Venmo. This was a whole new way to pay people. And nothing is more anxiety producing than money. So Venmo made their symbol emojis. It made payments personal and friendly, which took the anxiety out. You're new to the neighborhood and you know the last owner of your house had let the yard become overrun with weeds and trash. Your symbol might be a perfectly manicured lawn or a window box that is always well tended. If you are launching a new product, what problem does it solve? Recently at our firm, we got a new expense system that allows us to do our expenses from our phones. What got us to buy in to it? A picture of the wrinkled receipts we were always trying to smooth out and scan when we got back to the office after a long business trip. Problem solved. No receipts. Symbol. Image. Sold.

2. What symbolic gesture can you make in order to under-score your point? How do you define what your symbolic gesture is or could be?

    a. If you are changing perceptions, what is an action that you have recently taken or could authentically take? Again, if you are new to the neighborhood and are try-ing to counter the former tenant's slapdash yard care, a great symbolic gesture would be a handwritten note letting your neighbors know how much you admire their lawn and asking for advice on how to make yours look the same.

    b. If you are trying to establish your position for the first time, think about the actions you have taken or could take that will illustrate your pillars. When Oscar Health Insurance launched in 2012, they sent every new member a Fitbit and gave them discounts on their premiums if they attained 10,000 steps a day. It was a symbolic gesture that said, "We reward you for part-nering with us on your health," better than words alone could have communicated.

The bottom line is that pictures are worth a thousand words. And the more we can make our point with a visual that underscores our message, the more impactful and memorable it will be. Because often it's the negative images that stick with us. Our job in persuasion is to replace those negative images with positive ones. To change the nar-rative. To turn the page.

8

PERCEPTION OVER WORDS

Storytelling is the most powerful way to put ideas into the world today.

—ROBERT McKEE

Story is a key way we process and remember information and one of your most powerful tools. Everything we have covered (simplifying your message to *one* thing supported by three pillars and bolstered by streamlined proof points—and now pulling out stories) is a tool that makes it easy for the listener to remember. We are working to leave a lasting imprint. One that will stick with our target audience over time. Think about this: A week from now, when someone asks you about reading this book, you might stumble over relating the nine steps of the persuasion process, but you'll remember some random illustration I've shared almost verbatim. You'll be able to tell a friend how PharmaCare rebranded itself or how I started my career. Some arc with a beginning, middle, and end will be the nugget you take away, possibly for the rest of your life. Stories make facts "sticky," meaning memorable. And memorability is one of the keys to persuasion. Because when your position, brand, or product is memorable, you turn your audience into your PR machine and they start to do the work for you. That's when you catch fire.

Storytelling for brands and corporations is a big business now, and there is good reason for that. I recently had the opportunity to speak with Paul Smith, author of *Lead with a Story,* and he shared with me why it is so important. He said, "Storytelling makes the things that you're telling people much easier to remember. It helps build strong relationships because it gives your buyer or your audience time to just relax and listen to you, instead of being caught up in critical evaluation of everything you're saying. And stories are contagious. People will spread stories, but they won't spread a memo or a PowerPoint presentation." I couldn't agree more.

What storytelling is meant to do is demonstrate something that we couldn't otherwise say about ourselves without sounding disingenuous or boastful, like "I have your best intentions at heart" or "I'm a great mom."

When you have strong stories, which you will learn to craft in this chapter, your Persuasion Plan will always be anchored. Your audience will be more relaxed and engaged. Even if they try to push back, your stories will tether you. You can always come back to your stories because you can be assured that they will help move your argument forward and make your message more interesting, engaging, and relatable.

I have a friend who was a nurse for many years before she felt the pressure to get an advanced degree to become a nurse practitioner so she could buy a bigger house and gain access to the American dream. However, she wasn't happy. Her hours were relentless, she was never home to enjoy her new house, and her own health was suffering. She realized she needed to persuade her old hospital to take her back. But there was still a little lingering bitterness about her departure. To overcome that sour taste, she was going to need to make a strong case. I encouraged her to use story to bolster her master narrative, "Back and better able to serve."

"What I miss," she said, "was how my fridge looked when I worked here." This is a good disarming opening that grabs people's attention. "No, really. I always had the florist thank-you cards from patients all over my fridge, and they made me smile every morning before work and as I ended my day. In my new job, I don't have continuity of care with my patients. I see people for fifteen minutes and move them along. I miss the relationships."

The story, with its central symbol of the fridge covered in florist cards, said, "I was great at my job; my patients loved me," without her having to say it. Again, it's memorable and visual.

To be successful, stories must follow a certain formula. They should open with a compelling hook. Find a provocative way to introduce your story so that your audience pays attention, something like my friend's saying she missed how her fridge looked. The second component of a successful story is emotional appeal. You want to go back to your audience core's values, their emotional needs, and look for a story that elicits those emotions. Then you want to end your story with scalable facts that are going to reiterate your proof points.

Here is one of my favorite ones in the industry: "How do you kill a Toyota? A couple of years ago a show called *Top Gear* set out to kill a Toyota pickup truck. They strapped it down in the ocean during high tide. After eight hours in the salt water, they pulled it out and it started. They beat it with a wrecking ball, and it started. They set it on fire and let it burn for a while, and it still started. In one last attempt, they parked it on top of a 240-foot building that was being blown up with TNT. After digging it out of the rubble, they still got it to start. Even if our customers don't put their Toyotas through these challenges every day, we'd like them to know that if they do, we've built them to survive. Eighty percent of all Toyotas sold in the U.S. over the past twenty years are still on the road today."

The story opens with a counterintuitive statement that grabs your attention. It addresses their audience's obstacles and core values. Then this car becomes the main character, and as the challenges mount, you're rooting for the car. But what makes it a perfect story is that they didn't just leave it there. Because then the audience could have said, "Well, is it just the one truck? What are you trying to say?" That's why they included the fact that 80 percent of the cars that have been sold in the last twenty years are still on the road. It's now interesting, relevant, and scalable. It's telling a bigger story.

To summarize, for a story to be effective, it must be four things:

1. Interesting to your audience.
2. Connected to the core emotions we discussed in chapter 3.
3. Relatable.
4. Scalable, meaning it must be reflective of a bigger point you are trying to make.

Now I'm going to break down each one and share examples of stories that connected—and a few that didn't.

INTERESTING TO YOU DOESN'T MEAN INTERESTING TO THEM

A few years ago, after working on a water initiative in India, a beverage company came to us because they wanted to make one of their pillars a commitment to being water neutral by 2025. At first I wondered, *How can a soda company be water neutral?* But then I learned that they owned several healthier brands. Now our challenge was how to get their audience to care about the company's commitment to being water neutral and have people want to support that by picking the company's products over their less sustainable competitors.

So we started meeting with people who worked at the company to gather proof points and begin our persuasion process. First, we learned from a man who worked at the company's potato chip brand that they are actually the number one grower of potatoes in China and the United States. What they found is that, in the process of getting the potato to release its water, so it can be fried, they were actually generating a tremendous amount of water, which they now reuse at the plants so the factories don't have to use any outside water to make a potato chip.

This was an interesting, smart, and counterintuitive story. First, people don't think of potatoes and soda. Second, they don't think that there are ways a beverage company can actually be *generating* water in their product pipeline, but the company found one.

One of my colleagues was walking on the plant floor of an auto manufacturer and he noticed that everybody was wearing sweatbands. He asked, "Why is everybody wearing sweatbands?" They answered, "Oh, we cover our watches and wedding bands with sweatbands because you don't want to scratch the car."

My colleague said, "Well, why aren't you telling that story to illustrate your attention to quality?"

They answered, "Because every auto manufacturer does it. It's not new, it's not interesting."

My colleague countered, "But you're trying to make the point that you pay attention to detail, and nobody else knows that this is common practice. If you're the one that tells that story, you're going to be the one that gets the credit for it."

Don't be reluctant to tell a story that might seem obvious to you.

Clients are frequently hesitant to share stories that are obvious to them, but when you remember that you're trying to persuade people of something that they don't already know, it's actually vital to introduce them to the ideas that you take for granted.

When you're persuading, either your audience knows nothing about you or they have a different opinion entirely about you than you do about yourself. Any story that you might take for granted should be fair game. What you want to be able to check it against is not whether you think it's interesting but whether you think that person will have had that kind of experience themselves or have heard anything like that before.

That can go in both directions, because for a politician you want a story that is a connection point, one that makes the voters think, *I also have a grandchild, I also worked hard to make something of my life.* It doesn't necessarily have to be revelatory; it just has to be authentic and relatable. Ronald Reagan was the first president ever to bring individual citizens into the State of the Union address, saying, "I met this person on the road. She is why we're fighting hunger; he is why we're fighting the war on drugs." Now it's become standard operating procedure—because it works. But one word of caution we give our clients: You must be careful that the stories don't come off as rote. These should be real.

If you're trying to convince somebody to come work for you, that you're a great company, what better way than telling stories? If you know that person has young kids, you probably want to tell him or her a story about how your company supports you to find that balance, or how somebody down the hall isn't here today because her daughter has a recital, or the boss leaves every night at six P.M. so that he can have dinner with his kids, then goes back online. You're illustrating the point that this is a family-friendly place to work. It's not just story for story's sake; it's to illustrate your point, to reinforce your master narrative and your three pillars.

Just because this story is a routine part of *your* life doesn't mean it's boring to your audience. Story is what brings everything to life.

EMOTIONAL

To be effective in persuasion, all stories should tap into a core emotion. They do this by following certain rules developed over thousands of years that work with what our brains find satisfying. From Aristotle's *Poetics* to Joseph Campbell's *The Hero with a Thousand Faces*, much has been written about what we require of a narrative as an audience to find it resonant. Stories must have an arc, with a beginning, middle, and end. There should be a protagonist. A struggle for a clear object of desire. And a resolution. When it comes to persuasion, though, we need to be mindful of a few more criteria.

First, you must be specific. If a pharma company says, "We cure disease," it's vague and hard to connect to. Instead if they say, "This is a man with HIV celebrating his eightieth birthday," or "This is a woman with cancer who is going to live to see her three children grow up," or "Thanks to our vaccine, this child is protected against measles," then the audience can see themselves in the patient. If you say you envision a world free of disease, that's too ambitious. That also goes against the idea of the incremental change that's important to persuasion. Instead, if you say, "We've allocated 80 percent of our research to tackling our most daunting diseases like cancer, Alzheimer's, and heart disease," you're going to be in a better place.

The second key is deciding who the hero of your story is going to be. Is it you, the company, or the product? This isn't always obvious at first. But as you pick your stories, think about this: You should always create a protagonist that audiences can feel empathy for. If they can recognize themselves in that character, then ultimately they are rooting for themselves. This is something that Robert McKee talks about in his book *Storynomics*. When you pick your stories, they don't always have to feature you or your company. In fact, not all of them should. While you definitely need to have stories about yourself, you also need to have stories about and from other people, or you're going to be really limited in the stories you can tell.

Then decide who the hero is going to be. For example, when we were working with a pharmaceutical company, it was as important to decide who was going to tell the stories as the message themselves. We found that the message was *much* stronger coming from the employees—specifically the scientists—than from the executives.

The third key is going back to your audience's obstacles and values. When you say something like "Invention drives us," that's about you, so that doesn't address their obstacle of thinking all you care about is yourself. If their biggest problem with you is that they think that you're greedy and profit drives you, they're going to say no right off the bat. If we're told something that completely competes with what we believe, our brain is going to shut down.

For PharmaCare, that emotional connection was critical, so we needed to lead with stories that humanized the brand. The master narrative was, "Exploring for cures; adding years to your life and life to your years," and we told the story of a little boy who grew up in New Jersey and became a chemist who discovered an antibiotic in the Pine Barrens of his home state.

RELATABLE

In the movie *Planes, Trains and Automobiles*, Steve Martin says to John Candy, "You know, when you're telling these little stories, here's a good idea: have a point. It makes it so much more interesting for the listener!" It's funny because it's true. We've all been on the receiving end of a story that seemed to have no point.

Frequently we go into companies who have done these amazing story projects and have beautiful examples and anecdotes about who the company is and what it stands for. But unless these are all packaged up together with the work we did in chapters 5 and 6 to keep coming back to their audience's needs, values, and obstacles, they can fail to support your objective and miss the mark.

An example of one company that wanted to avoid exactly that is Hershey, which had started an incredible nutrition initiative in Africa. They wisely wanted to preempt any backlash that could result from not starting with the millions of undernourished kids here at home. We realized they needed to lead with their story: "In the early 1900s Milton Hershey opened a school for underprivileged children in Pennsylvania; this new initiative is following in that history." We made sure that every speaking point started with what they do for kids at home, from their backpack program in St. Louis to their partnership with Rise Against Hunger. This new work in Africa needed to be seen as just the latest chapter in the story of Hershey's taking care of children.

A few years ago, at the AutoCo plant in Kentucky, a beloved team leader was diagnosed with breast cancer. Because of the cancer, she was forced to take medical leave so that she could have a mastectomy. On her last day of work before going to surgery, over 90 percent of the team members and management at the Kentucky plant wore pink shirts and ribbons to show their support. They wanted her to know that the AutoCo family was thinking about her and fighting the cancer with her. To this day, team members talk about how moving it was.

Now, that's a very interesting story, but it didn't tie to what we were trying to convince people of, which is that AutoCo makes cars for how you live. If you're trying to persuade somebody that AutoCo is a good place to work, that would be different. It's a great example of a compelling story that doesn't make the cut because it doesn't lead up to a pillar or the master narrative.

Here's an example of a story that is relatable and relevant. When we were working with AutoCo on their third pillar, *together*, we knew that people didn't know the community-service side of the company. So we were trying to find the right story that would underscore this. They shared their know-how with small businesses and nonprofits, helped ERs be more efficient and post-disaster home rebuilding to happen faster. But the specific story we went with was:

"At AutoCo, we believe that a thriving community supports all consumers. That's why we share our expertise with North American organizations in need of extra support. For example, a U.S. pipe and fittings manufacturer, a small business, was losing market share to foreign countries. It faced the prospect of relocating to lower labor costs or closing altogether. We had our engineers partner with them to improve productivity, lower costs, and improve quality, all with no layoffs.

"Now they are growing and exporting their products to more than a hundred countries. They are just one of more than twenty companies that we are helping today, with a commitment to work with forty organizations each and every year."

Now the story has a stronger message that ties to the audience's *Why do I care?* Because AutoCo is helping keep jobs in the United States, and that feels like a relatable win for their consumers, one that they want to support.

SCALABLE

There is one major caveat to using stories, though. They must be scalable and representative of something that is truly important to your audience. For example, we have a lot of clients in pharma who want to tell heartstring-tugging stories about one of their patients who survived against all odds because of a clinical trial. But what we've found when we test those ads is that people ask, "Was that just the one patient? Are you cherry picking, or is this representative of something bigger?"

I can remember in 2009 when we were talking about a bank's trying to restore communities where there had been a lot of foreclosures. They had a voluntary day of service where employees went in and helped refurbish houses in which there had been vandalism because of abandonment. What I found interesting was that when we told the story in focus groups, people responded, "Well, now the bank is taking credit for what their employees did. Their employees felt so bad to be working for the man that they went out and did this."

So instead we said, "We have a commitment to helping everybody who lost a home find a home, and we have set up offices throughout the country that will help place people in homes, and here is one story. Roger Johnson served in Iraq. When he came back home, low interest rates made investing in the American dream a reality for him. But when his old injuries flared up and he had to go on disability, he was unable to repay his fluctuating loan. But thanks to our refinance program and home placement service, we have found Roger and his family a new place to live near his new job. So far we have put 17,000 people back in homes this year." Then the story is part of a more powerful narrative.

At AutoCo, we could have just said, "We're the first company with adjustable back seats," but how does that connect to the consumer? Instead we said, "Every one of our engineers spends two years on the road studying how you use our cars. It takes 7,000 engineers to make this one car." That sounds much bigger than just that one story.

For pharma companies, we have learned we have to say, "Here's one patient right now who is cured, *and* we currently have four hundred clinical trials with 73,000 people in them." Then that cured patient becomes not just a one-off, but part of something that's measured and real.

When we think about the Muslim American example that we talked about earlier, if I told you a beautiful story about a third-generation veteran who was Muslim, you could say to me, "That's one. What does that prove?" Instead, if I told you, "In fact, there are 10,000 active military personnel right now who are Muslim and there's one that I am friends with who is third generation in this country. He's got three kids. The reason he enlisted was that after September 11 he was so upset that this threat had happened to our country in the name of his religion that he said he had to enlist." Now you've got a story that weaves in the theme of safety and the proof point of participation by Muslim Americans in the armed forces; it also puts a compelling beginning, middle, and end on it. Then the story becomes part of a debate.

I find all the time that if I say in Democrat-centric New York City, "The characterization of Trump supporters is unfair. Let me tell you about my brother," people respond, "Okay, so you know one. What about the rest of them?" I'm more persuasive if instead I say, "Over the last three years I've spoken with thousands of Trump supporters, and what I've found is that they want the same things that you want: jobs and hope. For example, my brother has had it tough for a long time—the financial crisis took a toll on his career. He had lost hope and really felt excluded and forgotten by most all politicians. Donald Trump gave him hope. I know there are hundreds of thousands of people across the country who are in the same place, whether they're living around factories that have closed or whether they're in an industry that shut down. And we would be foolish not to listen to them. Supporting Trump doesn't make them bad people; it makes them human."

If I'm trying to persuade Democrats to reach out to Trump voters and try to empathetically, authentically address their needs and remove their obstacles, I would tell them to focus more on jobs. They could think about someone like my brother, and share why their way is a better way to provide jobs and why it will get more people back to work.

WINNERS

7-Eleven asked us to help them persuade people that they could get fresh local sandwiches at a place more famous for packaged, processed fare. They had reached out to local vendors to start selling their sandwiches at 7-Eleven, but they needed a symbol and a story to persuade the customer. The symbol we hit on was a sign above the sandwiches that read: MADE THIS MORNING. DROPPED OFF BY ___, and the name of the local farmer who made them. Then we needed to tell the story of the local person who was making the sandwiches to counter the fact that consumers thought they came from a factory or were made four days ago somewhere. The network of farmers became the face of the campaign.

Here's another example: L'Oréal wanted to showcase some of their smaller boutique brands and the entrepreneurial spirit that still exists in the company. It helped to both draw new customers and inspire employees to want to come work there. So they chose to make the face of L'Oréal the founder of one of their brands, Lisa Price. She founded her business in her Brooklyn home, where she developed lotions and hair products and sold them in neighborhood markets. In video ads, Ms. Price, who is still involved with the company, rides an escalator at L'Oréal's New York office. Images show Ms. Price at a kitchen stove, alongside her mom, and finally on Oprah Winfrey's show. The camera then pans to a trophy commemorating L'Oréal's acquisition of Carol's Daughter at the end of 2014. In the video, which ran on social media, Ms. Price says, "I actually got to watch a dream come true." Other stories in this initiative include the beauty brands Urban Decay, IT Cosmetics, and Seed Phytonutrients, featuring the founders of those brands, who are still involved. Matthew DiGirolamo, the chief communications officer of L'Oréal USA, makes the point that these stories are proving to be a more powerful marketing message than many of the other more traditional approaches they have taken.

CONCLUSION

Whether you are interviewing for a job, advocating for an issue important to you, or building a brand, you should have at least one anecdote at the ready to prove your point, illustrate the pillars of your master narrative, and bring color to the people you are talking to. So how do you find it? You go back to your master narrative. To your proof points. To your symbol. You find an anecdote that illustrates what it is that you uniquely deliver. While this might sound extreme, Paul Smith says that, "You literally need to have hundreds of stories in your repertoire, like arrows in your quiver, ready to tell at the right moment depending on what the situation is."

The exercise you need to go through now is to choose your stories. Remember, we connect through stories; we don't connect over facts. We don't share facts around the fire. Go through these steps, checking against your master narrative and each of your proof points. Find the stories that best illustrate your argument. Sometimes the story is how you decided to change careers. Sometimes it's a story about how you solved a similar challenge for someone else. Sometimes it's a story to illustrate your commitment to community. What is the personal, authentic story you're going to tell to make your master narrative memorable?

PART 5

OWNERSHIP

9

PERSUASION IN TRAINING

It's not what you say, it's what they hear.

—MASLANSKY + PARTNERS TAGLINE

Now you have your *draft* Persuasion Plan. This is your foundation, your starting point. But until you know how people are going to react to it and how you will react using it, you can't go any further. I have seen this happen time and time again. You have the message. You have it practiced. You have it ready. Then the time comes to persuade someone outside your test circle, and it all falls flat. Recently I was watching a CEO be interviewed on a morning show panel. He clearly had his talking points, the ones he thought were going to persuade people to reinvest in his company by bringing consumers back to his brand. It was clear that his master narrative was that his food company was innovative. No matter what question he was asked his answer was "We are just going to innovate and make our foods taste better." It was painful to watch. I don't know if he just wasn't prepared or didn't have permission from his legal team to talk about anything other than innovation. But the interview was a disaster.

And googling his name later, I found he was no longer CEO of that company.

The point of that story is this: A Persuasion Plan on paper is just a plan. You don't yet know how it will feel coming off your tongue. You don't yet know how your target audience will react. You don't yet know what questions you will get. That's why this phase is all about practice. Role-play. Simulation. Testing. Refining. Call it what you will, but you have to be *sure* that the message you developed is going to have the impact that you want it to have. This is what I recommend: If you have the budget, call me. I am happy to help. If you don't want to call me, call a research firm. If you don't have any budget, find three to five people who are truly representative of your target audience and ask if you can take them to coffee, lunch, or drinks and run some ideas by them. If you are looking for people outside your typical circles, social media can be hugely helpful. Put out a notice that you are looking to FaceTime or talk with people who fit a specific criterion—for example, "I am looking for women age fifty-five to sixty who still have school-age children in the home." I promise that even if you don't know them, you know someone who knows them.

Also consider asking a friend who might be like-minded to your target audience if they would be up for role-playing. Let's say you want to persuade your in-laws to pull back on giving your children so many gifts. Using a friend or colleague in their demographic might help you see the issue from their point of view and prepare your points.

This is where the rubber meets the road. While we have prepared as best as we can, it's not until we see our messages come to life in the real world that we can truly understand how they'll land.

LEARNING IN THE ROOM

We were hired by a medical device company to persuade heart surgeons to switch to a new valve replacement. Prior to this company's invention, there were only two kinds on the market, a natural heart valve and a mechanical heart valve. Both came with trade-offs. The natural ones, typically bovine or porcine, wore out faster, necessitating additional surgery every ten or so years. The mechanical ones lasted longer but necessitated being on blood thinners for the rest of your life, which came with its own set of risks.

This company was introducing an innovative heart valve that wouldn't wear out or require blood thinners. It was backed by great studies and was a total game changer. We were so excited to go out and talk about it because we thought it would sell itself. But when we talked to surgeons, they unequivocally said, "Nope, don't want it."

Our master narrative and language strategy had fallen completely flat.

Stunned, we took a break after three sets of the interviews to debrief with the client. We were discussing why the language strategy wasn't working and kept talking about how difficult it was to break through to doctors. Because of their years of training, they always seemed to know better. We struggled until we took a step back and tried to have empathy for them. Why couldn't they hear our message? What was the obstacle? We decided that we had to make it the doctors' idea. We couldn't force the message on them.

The new problem was, that conclusion was based on our preconceived notions about the doctors. We knew from experience that you cannot build empathetic, persuasive language strategy from a place of judgment. So what else could it have been?

We went back to the drawing board, pushed ourselves to stay

curious, and started parsing the newly collected data. It suddenly occurred to us, *Maybe they're afraid of trying something new.* It turned out that was it. The doctors didn't want to try something they perceived as risky on a patient entrusting them with their lives when they had something that was proven.

Everything that we were communicating—that this was brand-new, innovative, and game-changing—made them think that it wasn't proven. They had confidence in the procedures and valves they'd been using.

What we realized was that we needed to take out all the language emphasizing the newness of it, while still conveying that this was something totally life-changing for the patients. We went back and tested new language, and what the doctors responded really positively to was *breakthrough*. We couldn't figure it out. Afterward we asked, "Why could you be okay with *breakthrough* but not *innovative*?" What we learned is that penicillin is still referred to as a "breakthrough" drug, even though it's not new. So in the medical world, a product or procedure can be a "breakthrough" and still be safe.

The valve went on to revolutionize heart surgery. You can think all is lost in these moments. But if you stay curious instead of giving up, the key might reveal itself in the room.

QUESTIONS TO TEST YOUR STRATEGY

What follows is a rundown of the questions you should ask these people when you connect with them. Most of these should sound familiar because they summarize many of the steps we have gone through to get here.

A BASELINE POSITION

Before you even begin the conversation, you want to know where the person is coming from with regard to this issue. Then find out why they feel the way they do. Once again, you must stay neutral and curious during this part of the interview.

1. **Current beliefs.** Before you start, ask the person what their current beliefs are about the issue, product, company, or position. Don't critique their response. Just listen.

2. **Why do they believe or think that?** Ask them why. What is their experience with the topic (if any)? What have they heard? What has influenced them? Where do they get their information? How much does it impact their daily life? What matters to them about this issue?

WHAT THEY HEAR

Then ask them to listen to you and hold any thoughts until you finish. As you're speaking, have them write down any questions or comments on a piece of paper for afterward.

Walk them through your persuasion points.

Then ask them the following questions and have them write down the answers before you discuss their responses.

1. **What did you hear?**

   Without any comment, ask the person to repeat back to you what they took away from the message. We often say

191

at our firm that it's not what you say that matters, it's what they hear. So you might find that even though you thought you were saying one thing, your audience was hearing quite another. That is why this is an exploratory phase. We can often learn things here that surprise us. Sometimes it's a little thing. For example, a while ago I was working for an asset manager who wanted to talk about their customized investment solutions. I found out that a lot of folks didn't like the word *solutions* when it came to investments. Why? When they heard the word *solution*, they heard that they have a problem, which implied they had been mishandling their money. It came off as subtly insulting. Separately, investors also told me that a solution is one point in time. And consumers wanted something that lasted for the long term. What they embraced was the word *strategy*. Surprising, right? But true. Sometimes it's that small. Sometimes it's much, much bigger.

2. **Does this message matter to you? If so, why? If not, what does matter?**

You want to know that something about this message is relevant to your target audience. If there isn't anything meaningful in the message, they will not do anything with it. You will be lucky if they remember it in a week. So it's important to make sure that you aren't just sharing a message that matters to you. You are sharing one that matters to them. Sometimes it can be a subtle shift that makes all the difference. For example, you might have said, "I have the right experience for the job." To the person you are talking to, that might not matter. They might have twenty people in the waiting room with the right experience. But if you say, "I have done this before, and I can do it again in a way that will take work off your plate," that turn of phrase might make all the difference.

3. What will you do differently, if anything, as a result of this message?

Truly persuasive arguments will cause some sort of behavior or belief change. You might not get all the way where you want to go, but you do want to get them part of the way there. Double-check what they say they will do against your desired actions. Are you getting close? Are you making progress in the right direction? If not, make sure you ask them why. What's getting in the way?

4. What did you learn that you didn't know before?

We often say that anything that is ambiguous will be interpreted negatively. If someone learned something new *and* that something new is positive, you are likely moving in the right direction.

5. Are there any words or phrases that stand out to you in a good or bad way?

Let's face it, certain language carries baggage. Take, for example, the word I mentioned before: *moist*. I hate that word in every context. I don't want moist cake. Moist cookies. Moist anything. If I hear the word *moist*, I will run for the hills. Likewise, you might be triggering your audience with the simplest of terms.

6. What emotions do you feel when you hear this message?

Back in chapter 3 we talked about the Change Triangle. It's important to check to ensure you are striking a chord with people's core emotions. So have them check any of the following that apply and fill in the blanks:

a. I am angry at _____

   because _____.

b. I feel sad about _____

   because _____.

c. I am afraid of _____

   because of _____.

d. I am disgusted by _____

   for doing _____.

e. I feel joy about _____

   and feel like sharing it with _____.

f. I am excited about _____

   and want to share it with _____.

g. I feel anxious about _____

   because _____.

h. I feel ashamed about _____

   because _____.

i. I feel guilt about _____

   because _____.

After they have filled this out and you've discussed their response to your message, do not debate. Do not refute. Do not attempt to correct their opinions. Remember, it's your job to stay curious, not to pick apart their arguments; if you are inclined to argue with them, don't. Instead, ask them *why* they feel the way they do, or *why* they trust the resource they do, or *why* they do what they do. Remember what Dr. Jenny Susser said: asking questions helps blood flow in our brains so we can stay curious. While I realize you might not get overly heated when talking about why someone should buy one mutual fund over another, certain topics will trigger emotions on both of your parts.

So now you have completed your interviews. You have your data. If you passed with flying colors, go out there and get started. If you haven't, it's okay. This is a key part of the process. If this was easy, everyone would effortlessly be persuading each other of things all the time. Go back and edit your Persuasion Plan. Update your stories. Find the right proof points and gut check it again.

For some this will come naturally; for others it will take some practice. But don't be discouraged. Empathy and persuasion are both like a hard-to-train muscle. It will feel awkward to exercise it at first and it will hurt along the way. But you will learn, and once you do, it will become second nature.

ARE WE THERE YET?

It happens almost monthly—a client comes back to us and says, "We need to update our message," and we have to tell them, "No, you don't."

Typically they think it's time for an update for one of two reasons: things haven't moved for them as quickly as they hoped or, more commonly, they're bored. But we always say, "If you're not bored to tears with your message, you haven't even begun to penetrate."

In 2009, Tropicana hired the now defunct Arnell Group, a re-branding consultant, to overhaul their brand. Tropicana spent $35 million to redesign and promote their new packaging, and it was a disaster. The new packaging looked generic, which made people think Tropicana had been taken off the shelves, and worse, they were suspicious of the contents. It totally backfired. What the branding people didn't get was that their customers already *had* a strong relationship with Tropicana, as embodied by the Tropicana package. The "old" package was a signpost in stores, serving to help shoppers easily locate their trusted product. Their loyal consumers had what they wanted. That isn't the time to make a change.

Changing too frequently doesn't give the message a chance to penetrate or distribute. The value of repetition is that you're speaking not just so people will hear you but so they'll repeat your message for you. Studies show the person you're trying to persuade needs to hear your message three to five times before that can happen. They need to hear your master narrative enough that it crosses their synapses.

We know how to do this in our real lives. When we want someone to remember something, we repeat it over and over, regardless of whether we're enjoying it. "Don't forget to lock the door after we leave." "Take your medication on a full stomach." "No Instagram until you finish your homework." Like Trump, we keep the instructions simple, clear, and memorable, and we say them a lot. Disseminating branding language is no different.

The perils of changing up a message too soon is that it breaks trust. As Moshe Bar says in his book *Predictions in the Brain*, trust is about easy predictability. Breaking trust is a failure to meet the expectations you set up in people's thinking. Imagine your spouse getting a drastic haircut or buying a sports car without consulting you. It begs the question: *Wait, who* are *you? I thought I knew you, but now I'm not so sure.* If persuasion is dependent upon having your audience trust you, be sure you're not throwing away what you've already won. If you make yourself or your brand harder to predict, you make it less likely to be chosen.

We do an annual employee engagement survey, and two years ago we got feedback that we scored really high on everything except for "management shares information in a timely manner." As a response we could have just started sharing information more frequently, which we did. But the action alone wouldn't have changed the perception. We needed to send the message that we *learned* from the feedback. We needed to let the team know that we heard them and were committed to doing better. So Michael decided that at every Monday staff meeting he was going to have an "information in a timely manner" segment. Instead of saying, "This is what's going on this week," he said, "Here is the information in a timely manner." He repeated it over and over again, and the result spoke for itself. We went from scoring the lowest on that parameter to scoring the highest in one year. By repeatedly using the language, you make the audience feel heard and a shift happens.

WHEN YOU DO HAVE TO CHANGE

In this section I'm going to cover the three reasons why people do sometimes have to change their master narratives: a sudden contradiction emerges, language evolves, or the market gets too crowded and the narrative seems bland.

The most common reason is that a new language land mine or contradiction alert develops. It might be that at the time that you develop your Persuasion Plan, certain things are true, but then they change. For example, if you are an oil company that has stood on your environmental record and then a tanker of yours runs aground and you have a spill. Or if you manufacture hip replacements and have a good safety record, but suddenly a whistle-blower spreads the word that you make faulty devices. If suddenly there are contradictions in your ability to deliver on that narrative, it's got to change.

Then sometimes words change meaning over time. For example, we have a product called Wire Tap. It's a social media mining tool that we use to listen to conversations for language patterns. When we named it Wire Tap, the name was edgy in a fun way. Now the name sounds really upsetting and needs to be rethought.

Then you have markets that crowd themselves out. We worked with a financial services client years ago who wanted to differentiate themselves on convenience. So, we talked about how they had a branch on every corner. But once mobile banking was invented, the number of branches became less relevant. Then the message that resonated most was "Bank anytime, anywhere." Then three other competitors jumped in and used the exact same message: anytime, anywhere. So after working with the bank and testing it again, we identified a different and ownable way of talking about convenience: "Bank on your schedule, not ours."

We changed up their master narrative because they wanted to have a unique space when "anytime, anywhere" ended up becoming not distinctive enough and even started to feel a little bit flip. Like, whenever, wherever. That didn't make customers feel in control.

When you're doing a good job, you're going to get crowded in your space. Sometimes that's okay. Because if you're trying to persuade people to legalize gay marriage and everybody starts using your language, you're not going to want to shift it, because that was the goal. But if you're trying to sell a credit card and everybody in your space starts using your language, that's bad, because you want to be distinct and unique.

At its core the story doesn't have to resonate with us, it has to resonate with our target audience, so until we practice it, test it, get curious about how people react to it, we can never be 100 percent sure if it's going to work. You can't skip this step. It's as important as everything you have done so far to pull all these pieces together. Persuasion is a muscle. Building it takes discipline, practice, and repetition. But keep at it. It will be worth it when you get to the other side.

10

THE BIG TEST: PERSUASION IN CRISIS

Never let a good crisis go to waste.   —WINSTON CHURCHILL

Sometimes, despite everyone's best intentions, things go wrong. The product you're persuading people to buy is defective. People in your company behave badly. An ingredient you relied on is revealed to be harmful. You hit Reply All on an email your mother-in-law should never have received. Suddenly your brand is tarnished, you're on your heels, and you wish you had Olivia Pope on speed dial.

When a national news story breaks about a product literally blowing up, know that most likely sometime in the last twenty-four hours my phone rang. Correcting the record and repairing reputations—that is a core specialty of ours. We have steered many brands back from the brink of crises that in the moment seemed fatal.

YOUR FIRST INSTINCT IS USUALLY THE WRONG ONE

The critical first step? Before you react, you need to stop and think. I often say to my clients, if you are reacting, you aren't acting. Responding to these situations successfully requires calm. It requires outside perspective. And it requires a process for organizing your thinking. Which means, by necessity, you cannot be in an adrenalized fear state, which is called "fight, flight, or freeze" for a reason. Adrenaline makes you want to do one of the three, and none of those is the right response.

When I walk in the door of the command center, somebody in the room is invariably suggesting, "Deny, deny, deny." The very *worst* thing someone facing a crisis can do is deny and get defensive. That's because a defensive posture always repels. Think about how those kinds of responses work in your personal life. Think of a time when you perceived that you had been wronged. If your friend or partner responded with "No, I didn't," or "I did, but it's not a big deal," or worse still, "I did, but look at all the other awesome things I do," chances are that left you *angrier* than you were to begin with. None of those are winning strategies, and yet I see my clients want to use them every time. The problem with all of these responses is the same: They are true to the offender but not to the offended. None of them take into account the feelings or values that have been betrayed. Without that, no matter what you do, it won't gain traction.

First, hearing "No, I didn't," is a flat-out insult to your audience. Never, ever pretend a problem isn't happening, even if the truth is that there is no problem. If your target believes there is a problem, then there is.

In 2010, Pampers introduced a new line of diapers called Dry Max that were supposed to be thinner and twice as absorbent. Some babies had their first diaper rash after using the new product. Parents, of course, connected the rash to the thing that had changed—the diaper. Then they posted pictures of the rashes, and those went viral because some of them looked like chemical burns. Management's first response was that it couldn't be their fault because they had tested

4 million diapers with zero rash increase. They thought it must be something else the customers were doing or using. Parents, fearful for the health of their babies, wanted to know who was responsible. In this context, being defensive only served to reinforce the parents' suspicions.

It can be tempting to say, "No, it didn't happen," or "That was a rogue employee [or division]," but imagine hearing that from your babysitter when you come home to find your son has painted the drapes. No, she didn't personally paint the drapes, but you're going to need to hear more from her than "Not me." As consumers, we expect that the top tier of the corporation is accountable for the behavior and choices of everyone under them—be they loan officers, burrito makers, or flight attendants.

Now imagine a different response to the Pampers accusations. What if P&G had said: "To see a baby experiencing a rash is a difficult and unsettling thing, not only for the baby but also for the parent. Our job is to make sure that our products are safe for use on your babies and our babies, too. That is why we test millions of diapers to ensure that our ingredients give babies the protection you want from a diaper without causing rashes or irritation." This strikes the right balance of acknowledging the truth of the customer while also addressing their own reality.

On April 20, 2010, the largest marine oil spill in the history of the petroleum industry began in the Gulf of Mexico. It's estimated that more than 4.9 million barrels were discharged into the Gulf. It took nearly five months to contain the damage. At first, BP's communication about the spill backfired. They were dismissive and defensive. Early in the crisis, the CEO said that the amount of oil that was released was "relatively tiny in a very big ocean." And if that wasn't bad enough, by May 30, their communications were hurting more than they were helping. The CEO famously said at one point to the press, "I'm sorry. We're sorry for the massive disruption it's caused their lives. There's no one who wants this over more than I do. I'd like my life back." Yikes. In response, President Obama said in an interview, "If he was working for me, I'd sack him."

The "It's not that big a deal" and the "It's hurting me as much as it's hurting you" approaches were insulting to all of us who cared for both the wildlife and the livelihoods of those affected. The reality was that no one cared about the CEO's life. And they certainly didn't buy that this was a relatively small amount of oil. They wanted the situation to be addressed. For the company to own the mistake. To be assured that this would never, ever happen again.

So in June, BP started an ad campaign with the CEO's apologizing. It was met with skepticism and criticism. While some people appreciated the apology, most felt that it was inauthentic, scripted, and a PR stunt. They needed to see more from him then just a one-off message. Folks wanted to hear from people on the ground, and they wanted to see the actions that were happening to address the damage and the broader commitment to making this right—all things we teach our clients.

Over time it became clear that BP had gotten the message. If you go to the YouTube channel for BP, you will find more than a hundred ads that they released over three years. They learned what we often tell our clients—you can't just apologize once. You can't just put the message out there a couple of times and expect it to be finished. You must repeat it until you are nauseous. Instead of focusing on executives, BP focused on workers. Instead of being defensive and dismissive, they showed what they were doing to fix the impact. And instead of trying to show that it was all fine and done, they talked about their long-term commitment. And while some still criticize the advertisements, you can't criticize their impact.

Lastly the "I did, but look at all the other awesome things that I do" approach never works because that is just beside the point. It doesn't work at home when your partner forgets to do the dishes, and it definitely doesn't work for brands. When we were working with an organization that was sending a significant amount of money to Africa to help eradicate HIV while still having problems here in the United States, people got upset. We heard consumers say, "Wait, they have problems financially right here in the United States and are spending money on HIV in Africa? What are they trying to do? It's like a papal indulgence. You can't buy your way to a better reputation." All they wanted to hear was what they were doing to get their financial house in order here at home.

THE EQUALLY UNHELPFUL SECOND INSTINCT

Most people's erroneous second instinct is to hide behind a list of facts and try to correct the record. We've all done it. When you're accused of forgetting to pick up milk, you list all the things you *did* get at the store. When your new client presentation falls flat, you list all the new business you've landed. When the fundraiser doesn't hit its target, you list all the other revenue generators you spearheaded. The problem is that, while all of that may be true, none of it speaks to the current issue. We see this all the time at my firm. And because of it, we say that "the facts will not set you free."

So when you have these two instincts—either to dismiss the claim altogether or to solely lean into facts for your response, sit on your hands. Because to follow either of those tacks is to make the response about *us*, not about *them*. And that mistake is fatal.

I'm about to take you through what you should do instead that will speak directly to your audience and persuade them to trust you again.

OBJECTIVELY EVALUATE THE PROBLEM FROM *THEIR* PERSPECTIVE, NOT YOURS

To begin, get calm by returning to curiosity, the same as you did when you were getting to know your target audience. Once you've gotten calm, you must return to empathy. I find a tip that helps my clients when it feels like everything is on the line is to pretend the situation is happening to someone else; thus they can stay as objective as possible and start asking questions. The maslansky approach to crisis response is built on data from more than twenty years of message testing and behavioral science. Michael Maslansky has turned crisis response into a science. But in its simplest terms, it boils down to three key areas you need to address. The first is:

1. What is the impact?

The first question you need to ask is how personal or direct the impact of this crisis is. This way you will understand the level of empathy that your message should convey. The more personal the crisis, the more empathetic the message must be.

This goes back to Maslow's hierarchy of needs, which we covered in chapter 2. The most personal violations concern physical safety: failing brakes, defective hip replacements, E. coli outbreaks. These are the violations that consumers believe could happen to them personally, so these must be addressed swiftly and forcefully.

Then slightly less personal are issues that impact your consumers' community—foreclosing on homes, a safety violation at a local bank branch. If they can see themselves in the problem or imagine being impacted by the problem, you must acknowledge it at that level.

Least personal are violations that impact people your consumer will never meet, problems that are troubling but still somewhat abstract to them—a bad decision that cost the firm a lot of money, a factory far away that doesn't pay employees enough. These issues may still require a response, but because they are less personal to your audience, they require less empathy.

2. Why are your stakeholders being critical of you?

As I pointed out in the Pampers example earlier in this chapter, when consumers are harmed, they look for someone to blame. They think about other situations where people were harmed in the same way and quickly assign blame in their situation. Without even thinking, they tap into a set of beliefs about big business, your industry, your company, or your political affiliation. For example, when customers are harmed by a product, customers often instinctively say that the company puts profits over their safety. Or when a customer is harmed by a large organization, they assume that big companies abuse their power.

After looking at hundreds of crises, we found that there are four distinct categories of negative narratives: you don't care, you are being dishonest, you are abusing your power, or you are making things worse.

When you face a crisis, it is critical to understand which narratives are involved. Why are people being critical? If the underlying criticism of you is about dishonesty, then you have to focus on demonstrating that you are not hiding anything or trying to avoid providing information. If the criticism is that you don't care about customers or the environment, then you must frame your response in this context. In today's environment, what may seem like a small issue to you may feel like a big issue to your audience. That is because they are connecting your actions to these bigger narratives and the worst examples of similar behavior they have seen in the past. By seeing the issue through their lens, you can build a response that addresses their concerns, rather than sounding like you missed the point.

3. What actions are you taking to address the crisis?

When your flight is canceled or your package doesn't arrive on time and you call customer service, what do you want? Well, obviously you want them to make the problem go away. When that isn't possible, you probably want to know that the company is taking some action to address the issue. If the company apologizes but says they can't do anything to help you, how do you feel? Probably not great.

The bottom line: When bad things happen, we want to know the people we hold responsible are going to do something about it. We want action. As Maslansky says, "Showing is always better than telling."

For BP, what *did* work to repair their reputation and consumer confidence was going to Louisiana and saying publicly, "We caused this and we're devoting tens of millions to solve it and we're not leaving until every drop of oil has been cleaned up and the area has been restored." Own it and *then* share how you're fixing it.

AutoCo finally recovered market share when they said, "We have a complete commitment to safety. That's why we have, at every single one of our plants, at every single step, a safety officer." That might have always been true, so it isn't necessarily about taking a new action, but they had to demonstrate that they were taking an action that addressed the concern.

As we discussed in chapter 7, Starbucks closed for an afternoon when Howard Schultz returned so that every barista could learn to make the perfect cup of coffee. "We hear you, we respect your concern, and we are taking visible action to restore your confidence" is much stronger than just saying, "We have a renewed commitment to quality."

In your response sometimes it will be appropriate for you to institute new policies and procedures as a result of the issue. Other times you will launch a new set of initiatives. And there will be times where you won't do anything new—but will need to talk about what you are already doing to show your focus and that you understand what the concerns are.

KEEP LIVING THE STORY

Recently a prominent oncologist came to me because he was having a PR crisis. He had been baselessly accused of malpractice and a big newspaper had run the story before my client had been cleared on all counts. He didn't want to have to stoop to address the nonsense, so he ignored it—until his medical practice dropped by half. The article was the first thing that came up on Google searches, and he had done nothing to counter it.

His first instinct, going back to the top of the chapter, was just to talk about his patient volume, his success rates. He thought what was at stake was his reputation, but I encouraged him to look at himself from a patient's perspective. They were entrusting him with their life. That's what was at stake.

So what was going to rebuild confidence? Individuals telling stories about what they gained in his care. "I was walking the same night." "I didn't have any side effects from the surgery."

I asked him what actions he could take. Could he do pro bono surgeries? Chair fundraisers? Sponsor foreign medical students?

He appeared often on TV, so I advised him that in every interview he did—even on unrelated issues, like the ACA—he always had to bring it back to this message: "My life's work is to make sure no one dies from this cancer." Repeating the message might seem uncomfortable, it might get boring, but until business rebounded to pre-lawsuit levels, he had to stay the course, putting the experience, the values, and the perspective of the people he was trying to persuade ahead of his own.

The bottom line is that the consumer, not the brand, gets to decide when it's time to move on. Same with the constituent and the public official. It's just like the cheating spouse. The cheater doesn't get to say, "I'm tired of apologizing." Think of companies that have been embroiled in recent crises—an oil company after a spill, a financial institution after reports of fraud, a food chain after an E. coli outbreak. These companies need to apologize to their customers publicly and often.

We encourage clients to place ads apologizing, send emails apologizing; if possible, to call each impacted customer and apologize. Apologize in a banner on the company's website. All of this is the first step to earning back the trust of their customers.

Frequently, though, companies, like people, get tired of apologizing. Because, of course, anyone who has something to apologize for has been fired early on, and policies and procedures have been put in place to ensure nothing like this happens again. Thus the people left behind to apologize actually have nothing to apologize for, and they're tired of it. They're ready to turn the page. However, the customers are not. In order for this message to be remembered, it has to be repeated. Meaning the company needs to live and breathe the message at every interaction—and for a good while longer.

AN EXAMPLE OF GETTING IT WRONG

In 2016, the London transport authority decided not to renew Uber's license, which caused a plummet in valuation of Uber globally and threatened its solvency. It was just around the time a new CEO was appointed—and he did something that disarmed folks. He apologized. Dara Khosrowshahi's apology to the people of London was a refreshing change in tone for a company that previously hadn't ceded an inch of ground in defense of its aggressive growth strategies. However, while the statement was a step in the right direction, it showed that the company still has a lot of work to do. The following is a breakdown of his apology, with maslansky's analysis and our recommendations for what they should have said instead.

The Response	Analysis	What Dynamic Response Recommends
"We want to thank everyone who uses Uber for your support over the last few days . . . While Uber has revolutionized the way people move in cities, it's equally true that we've got things wrong along the way."	This should be an apology, not a sales pitch. The self-congratulatory language discredits the sincerity of the apology and feels disingenuous.	**Acknowledge your audience's perspective:** "While Uber has done much to empower citizens' mobility in cities, we've also made many mistakes along the way."
"On behalf of everyone at Uber globally, I apologize for the mistakes we've made."	A direct apology when people perceive you've done wrong is the right move.	**Apologize:** No changes needed.
"We will appeal this decision, but we do so with the knowledge that we must also change. We won't be perfect, but we will listen to you, look to be long-term partners with the cities we serve, and run our business with humility, integrity, and passion."	The actions do not directly address the criticism. We're left asking, "How?" The lack of concrete actions will do little to address the negative narrative that Uber puts its own interests first.	**Cite actions that align with the perceived wrongdoing:** "Most notably, we made a mistake in not doing more to create an open dialogue with the city and the TfL about how seriously we take the safety of customers. My top priority is to address this, and I will be boarding a plane to London to speak with the TfL and the mayor tomorrow. "I look forward to showing you how we are stepping up our safety requirements to ensure incidents like this do not happen again."

The Response	Analysis	What Dynamic Response Recommends
"Here in London, we've already started doing more to contribute to the city. Wheelchair vehicles are on the road and our Clean Air Initiative . . . You have my commitment that we will work with London to make things right and keep this great city moving safely."	These actions are disconnected from the issue. They can support direct actions around safety but are too prominent here.	**Cite room for improvement:** "We will work to regain our license, but we do so with the knowledge that we need to accelerate changes to improve safety and do more to contribute to the city. We know many in London depend on Uber. You have my commitment that we will work with London to make things right and keep this great city moving safely."

LEARNING FROM AN EXAMPLE

I'm not sure how many of you remember Marriott's data breach in 2018. But it was one of the biggest data breaches of all time, with up to 500 million customers impacted. The data at risk included email addresses, mailing addresses, phone numbers, passport numbers, and encrypted customer credit card information.

In their initial response, Marriott made the same mistake many companies in crisis make: They treated this like a crisis of facts rather than a crisis of feelings. They listed in clinical detail what they knew, what they didn't know, and what they were doing. What they weren't addressing was consumers' emotions. And emotions were running high. There was fear. There was broken trust. And there was skepticism. Until Marriott dealt with that, they couldn't win back customer and investor trust. Here's a look at what they could have done from the start to begin to rebuild trust.

Marriott's Actual Response	What Marriott Should Have Said
They distanced themselves from the issue by using the third person and focusing on Starwood.	**They should validate our concerns and acknowledge their shortfall.**
"Marriott has taken measures to investigate and address a data security incident involving the Starwood guest reservation database."	"When you use our website, your data should be secure. But on November 19, we discovered the Starwood guest reservation database had been breached by attacks going back to 2014. You trusted us with your information, and we let you down."
"The company recently discovered that an unauthorized party had copied and encrypted information, and took steps toward removing it."	
They buried the details that mattered.	**They should cite shared goals.**
"The information also includes payment card numbers and payment card expiration dates, but the payment card numbers were encrypted using Advanced Encryption Standard encryption (AES-128)."	"We know your first priority is to know how this attack may have affected you. [*XYZ*] data was taken—including encrypted credit card statements. We don't yet know how the attack happened and whether the encryption keys were taken, as well. We've launched a full investigation to find out, but in the meantime we're doing everything we can to make this right . . . "
"Marriott learned during the investigation that there had been unauthorized access to the Starwood network since 2014."	
They did describe steps they took, but stopped short of reassuring us.	**They should use the actions they took to reassure us.**
"We have established a dedicated website and call center to answer questions you may have about this incident."	"We've established a dedicated website and call center *so you can get answers to any and all questions you have about the incident.*"

Marriott's Actual Response	What Marriott Should Have Said
"Marriott is providing guests the opportunity to enroll in WebWatcher free of charge for one year."	"We're paying for any member who wants to enroll in the cybersecurity service WebWatcher *to help keep their information safe.*" "And we're going to be completely transparent about the results of our investigation *so you know everything we do about what happened and how we're going to keep it from happening again.*"
They restated their goal. "Today, Marriott is reaffirming our commitment to our guests around the world."	They should let us know they get the severity and tell us what's next. "The fact that this happened is unacceptable. And we're ready to do whatever we can to make sure it doesn't happen again. We'll continue to keep you informed about what happened and what it means for you as we learn more."

This situation underlines a core conflict for companies deciding what to do in a crisis. Explanation and justification are easy to fall back on, but ineffective.

Following this framework and process will help you manage through crisis the right way.

SUMMING UP

I've been asked over and over again if it's possible to persuade when the facts don't matter. I always answer without hesitation: absolutely. If you walk through these steps, you will be able to change hearts and minds. The most important thing I can share with you is this: Take your emotion and perspective *out* of it and get their emotion *into* it.

In the post-fact, tribal, identity-driven world we live in, persuasion is rare. Engaging with people with different opinions is becoming rarer still. So when you do connect in a meaningful way, it will have an impact. It will be refreshing. And it will work.

Take the time to get out of your comfort zone and you just might change some minds—and maybe even the world—in the process.

APPENDIX

Persuasion Plan Workbook

STEP I. GETTING CLEAR ON YOUR OBJECTIVE

1. What is your objective?

_____

_____

_____

2. If you are successful, what do you want people to do or believe as a result of your efforts?

_____

_____

_____

3. Whom are you trying to persuade? Who is your target audience?

_____

_____

_____

Your target audience's current belief:

└─► Desired belief or action of target audience:

YOUR MISSION STATEMENT

Be clear. Be bold. Be specific.

_____

_____

_____

_____

_____

_____

_____

_____

_____

_____

_____

_____

_____

_____

_____

_____

_____

_____

_____

_____

_____

_____

_____

WHAT DO YOU WISH YOU COULD SAY?

Stream of consciousness. No filter. No thought.
Just what you really want to say.

_____

_____

_____

_____

_____

_____

_____

_____

_____

_____

_____

_____

_____

_____

_____

_____

_____

_____

_____

_____

_____

_____

STEP II. THEM

ACTIVE EMPATHY IN PRACTICE

Interview people in your target audience. Play the role of curious reporter. If you find yourself jumping to conclusions or getting emotional, slow down. Ask questions. Remember, you can't be curious and emotional at the same time.

Values-Based Empathy Questions

- Care/harm: Which person, group, or company related to the topic do you think was wrong? Why do you think they did what they did? Why does it matter to you?
- Fairness/cheating: Do you think a person, group, or company was treated unfairly? Who was treated unfairly? Why do you think they did what they did? And why does it matter to you? Do you think that one group was treated differently from another?
- Loyalty/betrayal: Do you think a person's, group's, or company's actions were loyal to their pack? Do you think they showed any lack of loyalty? Why does this matter to you?
- Authority/subversion: Did a person, group, or company show a lack of respect for authority? Did they fail to act in a way that then caused harm or chaos? Who did it and why? Why does this matter to you?

- Sanctity/degradation: Do you think anyone violated standards of decency or did something that was perceived as "disgusting"? Who did? Why do you think they did? Why does it matter to you?
- Liberty/oppression: Do you think that someone was denied their rights? Who was? Why do you think they were? Why does that matter to you?

Behavior-Based Empathy Questions

- What do you think today about the issue/product/service?
- What is your experience with the issue/product/service?
- Where did you learn about it?
- Who have you talked to about this issue/product/service in the past?
- Who influences you in general?
- Where do you get your information?
- How will this issue/product/service impact your daily life?
- What matters to you about this issue/product/service?
- Are you open and receptive to new ideas? Why or why not?
- What is your *why* for your position?

Emotional-Based Empathy Questions

Pretend you're a reporter and you're trying to get a story about how this person came to feel the way that they do. What are the racial, gender, and socioeconomic factors that influenced them? Think of every possible variable that could apply to the topic—family of origin, childhood, first good experience or bad experience with the topic. It's called intersectionality, which is a jargony word in therapy, but it's the point at which all these possible variables influenced your audience to make them feel this way.

- Tell me a little bit about why you're interested in this subject.
- Tell me why you hold the position you do.
- Can you tell me more about that?
- When did you first feel that way?

STEP III. CONNECTION

AND A LITTLE BIT MORE ABOUT YOUR TARGET AUDIENCE...

List all of their barriers to believing your point of view about your issue/product/service.

_____

_____

_____

_____

_____

_____

_____

_____

_____

_____

_____

_____

_____

_____

_____

_____

_____

_____

_____

_____

_____

_____

List all the things that matter to your target audience about this issue, product, or service.

_____

_____

_____

_____

_____

_____

_____

_____

_____

_____

_____

_____

_____

_____

_____

_____

_____

_____

_____

_____

_____

_____

_____

List all the things that you can deliver on authentically and credibly.

_____

_____

_____

_____

_____

_____

_____

_____

_____

_____

_____

_____

_____

_____

_____

_____

_____

_____

_____

_____

_____

_____

_____

PILLARS

Step 1: List all of the proof points you can to support your perspective.

_____

_____

_____

_____

_____

_____

_____

_____

_____

_____

_____

Step 2: Cross off any that reinforce any of the negative beliefs that your target audience has.

Step 3: Circle any that align with what matters most to your target audience.

Step 4: Categorize.

Step 5: Fine-tune the language.

YOUR PILLARS

Pillar One:	Pillar Two:	Pillar Three:
Proof points	Proof points	Proof points
1.	1.	1.
2.	2.	2.
3.	3.	3.

MASTER NARRATIVE

Step 1: Write a sentence summarizing your pillars.

_____

_____

_____

Step 2: Take it through the five whys.

1. Why does it matter to them?

_____

_____

_____

2. Why does it matter to them?

_____

_____

_____

3. Why does it matter to them?

_____

_____

_____

4. Why does it matter to them?

_____

_____

_____

5. Why does it matter to them?

_____

_____

_____

Step 3: Check the sentence against your three lists and core emotions.

Step 4: Test it against the four *P*s.

Plausible
Positive
Personal
Plainspoken

Step 5: Rewrite your sentence.

_____

_____

_____

STEP IV. STORY

STORIES

1. What is the best anecdote and story you have to illustrate your master narrative?

_____

_____

_____

2. What is the best anecdote and story you have to illustrate your first pillar?

_____

_____

_____

3. What is the best anecdote and story you have to illustrate your second pillar?

_____

_____

_____

4. What is the best anecdote and story you have to illustrate your third pillar?

_____

_____

_____

FILLING IN YOUR PERSUASION PLAN

Your Master Narrative:		
Story:		
Pillar One: Proof points 1. 2. 3. Story:	Pillar Two: Proof points 1. 2. 3. Story:	Pillar Three: Proof points 1. 2. 3. Story:

MAKING IT VISUAL

Now take a look at it all together. Does the master narrative or any of the pillars lend itself to any visual language or symbols?

STEP V. OWNERSHIP

Sit down with someone or multiple people from your target audience to practice your message. Just remember to suspend judgment and remain curious. This is all information that's going to help you strengthen your narrative.

1. What did you hear?
Without any comment, ask the person to repeat back to you what they took away from the message.

_____

_____

_____

2. Why does this message matter to you, if at all?
You want to know that something about this message is relevant to your target audience.

_____

_____

_____

3. What will you do differently, if anything, as a result of this message?
Truly persuasive arguments will cause some sort of behavior or belief change.

_____

_____

_____

4. What did you learn that you didn't know before?

_____

_____

_____

5. Are there any words or phrases that stand out to you in a good or bad way?

_____

_____

_____

6. What emotions do you feel when you hear this message?

_____

_____

_____

Earlier in the book we talked about the Change Triangle. It's important to check to ensure you are striking a chord with people's core emotions. So have them check any of the following that apply and fill in the blanks:

  a. I am angry at _____
     because _____ .

  b. I feel sad about _____
     because _____ .

  c. I am afraid of _____
     because of _____ .

  d. I am disgusted by _____
     for doing _____ .

  e. I feel joy about _____
     and feel like sharing it with _____ .

  f. I am excited about _____
     and want to share it with _____ .

  g. I feel anxious about _____
     because _____ .

  h. I feel ashamed about _____
     because _____ .

  i. I feel guilt about _____
     because _____ .

ACKNOWLEDGMENTS

First, thank you to my agent, Lucinda Blumenfeld. You are a fierce advocate, and anyone would be lucky to have you in their corner. Nicola, my coach, you somehow have made the daunting task of writing this easy (well, maybe not easy, but . . .) and approachable. I don't know how, but you did. And along the way, thank you both for becoming friends. I hope this is just the start of our story.

Enormous gratitude to my editor, Marian Lizzi, and the whole team at TarcherPerigee for all your time and attention, for believing in the book and challenging me to make it better.

Thank you to Michael Maslansky. Maz, you took a chance on me, and I will forever be grateful. You believed in me and supported me through my career here, and I wouldn't be who I am or where I am without you.

Thank you to my dear, inspired, amazing colleagues at maslansky. You are the smartest group of people I know. Keith, Larry, Katie, Justin, Clint, Catherine, Nicole, Ali, and Sachi—thank you for your help getting these stories just right, for being my sounding board when I needed a second or third set of eyes, and for all of your support. Lee and Hana, thank you for all the crazy work you put in, both late nights and early mornings, that made all the testing possible. Abbey, Lindsay, and Kris, thank you for the moral support and help making all of this happen.

ACKNOWLEDGMENTS

Thank you to my clients. You give me the chance to learn more about the world every day. You've taught me that you can have the best of everything, but if we don't get the message right it won't matter. I feel lucky every day to help tell your stories.

Thank you to my former colleagues who have remained family to me—Phifer, Jenni, Jenn, we've traveled the world one focus group facility at a time, learned so much about the world and people, and ultimately about ourselves. I love to see you thriving where you are.

Thank you to my Shero Mentors (official and unofficial, current and past)—Barb, Barri, Sharon, Claire, Olivia, Kathi, Marjorie, Liz, Lisa, KVB, Marina, Janet, and Jessie: I don't think I have thanked you enough. Sometimes it's been a quick conversation, other times it's been long heart-to-hearts. Sometimes I'm guessing that you don't even know that just watching you navigate your careers, motherhood (or fur-mommahood), and lives has had such an impact. They say if you can see it, you can be it. Each of you has modeled a behavior that I treasure and aspire to have. Each of your unique contributions to the world has made me, and a whole host of other women, better.

Thank you, Frank. I know you didn't know how much I learned from you, but I watched. I learned. And I am so, so blessed by you and the friendship that we now have.

Thank you to my colleagues at Fox News. You gave me a platform when I was an outlier and a shot when I had no TV experience. Collectively, we went through some of the craziest times starting in 2015 but had a front-row seat to *Persuasion* in action, and if it weren't for the opportunities you guys gave me, I might have missed it. Lauren, Lauren, Lee, Amy, Kelly May, Gavin, Ainsley, Steve, Brian, and the whole current and past team at *Fox and Friends*, thank you all for the countless hours, blood, sweat, and tears (and sometimes laughter) that went in to creating the Pulse of the People. Thank you to Brandalyn, Giselle, Javier, and the entire hair and makeup team for making me a better version of myself and for proving what my GiGi taught me—that a little powder and paint makes a lady what she ain't.

Thank you to my colleagues at Fox Business. Maria and Dagen—getting to sit beside you every Monday a.m. is a dream come true. You are the best in the business. Beyond hardworking and so incredibly generous. And, Mitch, you aren't so bad either . . . Gary, thank you for all your support and super sharp insights. And Tami—where would we be without you?

For my girls—Vick, Kris, Sha, Marcy, Jess, Jackie, Susan, Jen, Trish, Alex, and Jill—thank you each for being the best friends a girl could ask for.

Thank you to my family. There is no doubt that we don't share the same opinions and perspectives, but I have learned from and listened to all of you. It's because of you that I learned the most essential part of persuasion—empathy, understanding, and respect. I love you more than words.

Thank you, Jackson, Jamie, Morgan, Timothy, Andrew, Patrick, and baby M—the next generation—for being unique and amazing. I am so blessed to have each of you in my life. If you want to see real and meaningful change, take the time to understand those you disagree with. It will make all the difference. And I just know each of you was made to be a changemaker in your own special way.

Thank you, Mom, Bobbeee, Grandma, Grandpa, Aunt Franny, Uncle Fred, Aunt Sherry, Andrea, Josh, and Dad. You supported my dreams, my quirks, and my passions. You saw the best in me. And you gave me the most important gift I have—my faith. I'm blessed beyond measure to have your love and support in life.

Thank you, John. You're the best big bro I could ask for. And you called it early. If you hadn't, I don't think this book ever would have happened.

Thank you to my husband, Drew. You've been there since the beginning of this journey. And while I know we certainly haven't always agreed, I have learned from you (even if I don't always say so in the moment). Now here we are in the year of Bs. A baby and a book. He parted the seas for us. Thank you for reminding me when things got hard that all I need to do is in Exodus 14:14: "Be Still." Prayers have been answered and how very blessed we are. I wouldn't have it any other way.

Lastly, in late-breaking news, to Madeleine. You changed everything for the better. I need to find a whole new lexicon to describe both how amazing you are and the love I have for you. You are proof that dreams do come true—and sometimes they are even better than you could have imagined. You are perfect just as you are. I'm so blessed to be your mom. "You are fearfully and wonderfully made."—Psalm 139:14.

RESOURCES

Ariely, Dan. *Predictably Irrational: The Hidden Forces That Shape Our Decisions*, rev. and expanded ed. New York: Harper Perennial, 2010.

Bream, Cris. *I Feel You: The Surprising Power of Extreme Empathy*. Boston: Houghton Mifflin Harcourt, 2018.

Brown, Brené. *Rising Strong: How the Ability to Reset Transforms the Way We Live, Love, Parent, and Lead*. New York: Random House, 2017.

Christian, Brian, and Tom Griffiths. *Algorithms to Live By: The Computer Science of Human Decisions*. New York: Picador, 2017.

Fosha, Diana. *The Transforming Power of Affect: A Model for Accelerated Change*. New York: Basic Books, 2000.

Glaser, Judith E. *Conversational Intelligence: How Great Leaders Build Trust and Get Extraordinary Results*. New York: Routledge, 2016.

Haidt, Jonathan. *The Righteous Mind: Why Good People Are Divided by Politics and Religion*. New York: Vintage Books, 2013.

Heinrichs, Jay. *Thank You for Arguing: What Aristotle, Lincoln, and Homer Simpson Can Teach Us About the Art of Persuasion*, 3rd ed. New York: Three Rivers Press, 2017.

Hendel, Hilary Jacobs. *It's Not Always Depression: Working the Change Triangle to Listen to the Body, Discover Core Emotions, and Connect to Your Authentic Self*. New York: Spiegel & Grau, 2018.

RESOURCES

Hetherington, Marc, and Jonathan Weiler. *Prius or Pickup?: How the Answers to Four Simple Questions Explain America's Great Divide.* Boston: Houghton Mifflin Harcourt, 2018.

Kahneman, Daniel. *Thinking, Fast and Slow.* New York: Farrar, Straus and Giroux, 2013.

Lakoff, George. *The ALL NEW Don't Think of an Elephant! Know Your Values and Frame the Debate,* 10th anniversary ed. White River Junction, Hartford, VT: Chelsea Green Publishing, 2014.

McKee, Robert, and Tom Gerace. *Storynomics: Story-Driven Marketing in the Post-Advertising World.* New York: Twelve, 2018.

Maslansky, Michael, Scott West, Gary DeMoss, and David Saylor. *The Language of Trust: Selling Ideas in a World of Skeptics.* New York: Prentice Hall Press, 2011.

Miller, William R., and Stephen Rollnick. *Motivational Interviewing: Helping People Change,* 3rd ed. New York: Guilford Press, 2013.

Patterson, Kerry, Joseph Grenny, Ron McMillan, and Al Switzler. *Crucial Conversations: Tools for Talking When Stakes Are High,* 2nd ed. New York: McGraw-Hill Education, 2011.

INDEX

Page numbers in **bold** indicate charts or tables; those in *italics* indicate figures.

INDEX

Lee Carter is president of maslansky + partners, a language strategy firm based on the single idea that "it's not what you say, it's what they hear."® Lee oversees a portfolio that includes *Fortune* 100 and 500 companies as well as prominent nonprofits. As a television news personality and researcher, she doesn't rely on traditional polling for her unique insights into U.S. politics; rather, she analyzes voters' emotional responses because the reaction matters, but the "why" behind it matters more. It was this approach that allowed her to accurately predict the results of the 2016 presidential election and primaries.